T0191294

"Besides being beautiful little hand-sized objects themselves, showcasing exceptional writing, the wonder of these books is that they exist at all . . . Uniformly excellent, engaging, thought-provoking, and informative."

Jennifer Bort Yacovissi, *Washington Independent Review of Books*

". . . edifying and entertaining . . . perfect for slipping in a pocket and pulling out when life is on hold."

Sarah Murdoch, *Toronto Star*

"For my money, Object Lessons is the most consistently interesting nonfiction book series in America."

Megan Volpert, *PopMatters*

"[W]itty, thought-provoking, and poetic . . . These little books are a page-flipper's dream."

John Timpane, *The Philadelphia Inquirer*

"Though short, at roughly 25,000 words apiece, these books are anything but slight."

Marina Benjamin, *New Statesman*

The joy of the series, of reading *Remote Control, Golf Ball, Driver's License, Drone, Silence, Glass, Refrigerator, Hotel,* and *Waste* . . . in quick succession, lies in encountering the various turns through which each of their authors has been put by his or her object. . . . The object predominates, sits squarely center stage, directs the action. The object decides the genre, the chronology, and the limits of the study. Accordingly, the author has to take her cue from the *thing* she chose or that chose her. The result is a wonderfully uneven series of books, each one a *thing* unto itself."

Julian Yates, *Los Angeles Review of Books*

The Object Lessons series has a beautifully simple premise. Each book or essay centers on a specific object. This can be mundane or unexpected, humorous or politically timely. Whatever the subject, these descriptions reveal the rich worlds hidden under the surface of things."

Christine Ro, *Book Riot*

. . . a sensibility somewhere between Roland Barthes and Wes Anderson."

Simon Reynolds, author of *Retromania: Pop Culture's Addiction to Its Own Past*

OBJECT LESSONS

A book series about the hidden lives of ordinary things.

Series Editors:

Ian Bogost and Christopher Schaberg

In association with

BOOKS IN THE SERIES

Skateboard

JONATHAN RUSSELL CLARK

BLOOMSBURY ACADEMIC
NEW YORK · LONDON · OXFORD · NEW DELHI · SYDNEY

BLOOMSBURY ACADEMIC
Bloomsbury Publishing Inc
1385 Broadway, New York, NY 10018, USA
50 Bedford Square, London, WC1B 3DP, UK
29 Earlsfort Terrace, Dublin 2, Ireland

BLOOMSBURY, BLOOMSBURY ACADEMIC and the Diana logo are trademarks
of Bloomsbury Publishing Plc

First published in the United States of America 2022

Cover design: Alice Marwick

Bloomsbury Publishing Inc does not have any control over, or responsibility for,
any third-party websites referred to or in this book. All internet addresses given
in this book were correct at the time of going to press. The author and publisher
regret any inconvenience caused if addresses have changed or sites have
ceased to exist, but can accept no responsibility for any such changes.

Library of Congress Cataloging-in-Publication Data

ISBN: PB: 978-1-5013-6748-9
ePDF: 978-1-5013-6750-2
eBook: 978-1-5013-6749-6

Series: Object Lessons

Typeset by Deanta Global Publishing Services, Chennai, India
Printed and bound in the United States of America

To find out more about our authors and books visit www.bloomsbury.com and
sign up for our newsletters.

In memory of

Mark Waters

(10.20.1966 — 1.17.2021)

who made this book better

and

Zack Pahl

(12.19.1982 — 3.22.2021)

who made my youth better

"I'll tell you one of the great activities is skateboarding. To learn to do a skateboard trick, how many times do you have to get something wrong 'til you get it right? And if you learn to do that trick, now you've got a life lesson. Whenever I see those skateboard kids, I think: Those kids are going to be alright."

—JERRY SEINFELD

CONTENTS

PROLOGUE
MEMORY SCREEN

Christmas, 1995

"It's a Rhythm."

As I stared wide-eyed at the gift I held in my hands, imagining the endless potential of what I could do on it, my brother Adam asked what kind of skateboard I'd gotten, the brand of board being an important component of a skater's repertoire. There it was, written on the deck in flashy letters: Rhythm Skateboards. When I came downstairs that Christmas and opened my presents, there was only one I cared about, and I spotted it easily: a bulky, awkwardly wrapped object, what is now referred to with a mix of nostalgia and pejoration as a Christmas Complete. The full set-up of a skateboard—the deck, grip tape, trucks, wheels, bearings, and hardware—costs somewhere in the $120 to $160 range, so kids usually receive their first ones on holidays or birthdays. I was ten years old, and this was my first skateboard.

Both of my older brothers had been skating for a year or two at this point. I was following in their footsteps, or, more apropos, following their pushes. I was the hey-guys-wait-up-me-too kind of younger sibling who wanted to tag along and participate and be one of the older kids. Skateboarding in '94 wasn't nearly as popular or pervasive as it soon became, so there weren't many skaters in my hometown of Pickerington, Ohio. But I was only nine, so it wasn't as if I was out in the streets looking for fellow skaters. All of which meant that for the first few months, I skated alone. In the piercing cold of the winter months, I skated in my garage or my basement. During the dry days in spring and the warm days in fall, I pushed up and down my driveway or at the nearby elementary school. I can't now recall too many particulars of this developmental period, but I remember the way it felt: a trick always seemed both possible and unimaginable, tantalizingly on the other side of my skill and yet beyond my ability to picture what it would be like, so that attempting and failing at the same trick over and over and over again didn't deter or depress me. Rather, each failure led me slightly closer to landing back on the board's grip tape. And when the moment finally came, when my feet somehow lifted a piece of wood into the air, flipping it or rotating it and bringing it back to its rightful position where it began, the whole of my weight returning to standing on top of it—there was nothing like it. You think of a trick (or see one in a skate video or done by a friend or sibling), and then you try it yourself. With each attempt, you amend the flick and pop of your feet, and get a little closer, a little closer. There are setbacks: sometimes, no matter how hard you try, you just can't seem to get your body or the board to *do the thing*, or else you just can't figure out what you're doing wrong. But then, one time, suddenly, something clicks and you've moved once again back toward completion, toward the elusive land. The process of learning a trick isn't a straightforward trajectory from not knowing to knowing. Instead, it's a messy, miasmic back and forth of *try* and *think* and *learn* and *fuck up* and *try again* and *get a little closer* and *fail a little harder* and *finally figure it out* and *land it once* and *then be unable to repeat it* and *then figure it out again* and *then land again* and then, *finally*, feel like you've got it. It's a labyrinth, really. It's a convoluted path. It's a rhythm.

* * *

Rhythm Skateboards was founded in 1995 by Felix Arguelles and lasted until around 2001 or so. When I first began writing this book, I searched long and hard—both on the internet and through family photos— for an image of my first deck to no avail. My memory only provided a vague recollection of the specifics of the artwork, but I knew it was primarily tan or taupe and had highlights of either purple or blue, something like that. For how important a skater's first board is (especially for someone who has skated for 25 years now), it struck me as strange that I couldn't recall with any more accuracy just what the hell it looked like. I found it odd, too, that a purchasable product from not so very long ago was pretty much impossible to find online.

Then it struck me that for much of skateboarding's history, skaters didn't think of what they were doing as *history* at all. There wasn't any foresight about preserving the story, recording the shifts and changes that were occurring, the innovations, the developments, the art of it all. These were young, usually outcast kids, who more than anything felt wholly apart from the kind of mainstream culture that might, you know, take some time to trace its rollicking progress via written records, libraries, halls of fame, college departments, historical archives, etc.

A consequence of this lack is that much of the history of skateboarding remains lost, and, moreover, the true essence of skateboarding—the murky magic that pushed it from fly-by-night fad to worldwide culture—has so far been relatively unexamined. In order to understand the truth of something and the lessons it offers, a version of the events needs to be related. Of course, no objective, official, and final narrative exists; there are as many histories as there are skaters. But we can't even scratch at searching for its meanings unless we grapple with its history. The scope of this project doesn't allow for anything as complete as a true history, so what I thought I would instead try to capture the spirit of skateboarding in all its nuance. I found five people who exemplify the various components of the world of skating and have taken their stories, their thoughts, their status in skateboarding to dive into its various aspects. I hope that collectively these five portraits of skaters will make up a whole portrait of skating.

This book was written entirely during the Covid-19 pandemic, which means its scope is somewhat limited. I intended to travel to numerous locations, attend contests, tour production facilities, and generally do all the necessary reportage for a lengthy text on a subject. In lieu of experiential narration, I've instead focused on the individuals I profiled, and from their histories found ways to cover as much as I possibly could. In some ways the pandemic's restrictions have improved the book in terms of its in-depth assessments of skateboarding culture. Had I been able to travel, the focus of the chapters wouldn't have been as pointed, and my interviews with my subjects wouldn't have been as intimate. Instead of relaying its history, I hoped to find something essential about skateboarding, an enterprise that has been embarked on in previous generations.

There's a classic skate video from 1987 called *The Search for Animal Chin*, directed by Stacy Peralta and featuring the Bones Brigade. It's technically a narrative film rather than a skate video, but it's not a particularly engrossing one. It's goofy and awkward and, as we'll see, racist, but it's a seminal entry into skateboarding filmdom. *Animal Chin* begins with Stacy Peralta, co-owner of Powell Peralta, watching a news story on TV. A reporter interviews a man named Alan Winters, a businessman played by Gerrit Graham (an actor who appeared in a handful of Brian de Palma movies). Winters owns Slash Skates, "the largest manufacturer of skateboarding equipment in the world," and he talks about skateboarding as if it's only meaningful because it yields hefty profits. (Reporter: "What is going on with skateboarding these days?" Winters: "About 300 million a year." Reporter: "Skaters?" Winters: "Dollars, homeboy.") Winters clearly represents a betrayal of the ethos of skateboarding, as he has no understanding of it at all. The reporter asks him what kids are looking for, and Winters says, "It's that death, gore, dismemberment, whole type of go-for-it type of thing. I mean after all, that is what skateboarding is all about." Peralta, indignant over this crass interpretation, throws his TV out of the window.

We're then told in text that appears on the screen that:

In the beginning…

A man named Won Ton "Animal" Chin bolted skates onto a two-by-four and became the first skater. He had fun. Others followed and a transportation revolution was born.

But one day dark forces began to invade the skateworld. Animal Chin was forced to go underground.

Then there are newspaper headlines and TV reports on Animal Chin's disappearance. So Tony Hawk, Rodney Mullen, Lance Mountain, and the rest of the gang set out to find this elusive figure, who represents the true meaning of skateboarding.

The character Animal Chin looks exactly how his racist name implies. He's a very old Asian man with a long beard sporting a conical hat, the stereotypical portrait of "ancient Chinese wisdom," and watching it more than thirty years later induces plenty of cringes. Pair this with the bad acting and the clunky writing, you end up with quite a bad movie. The skating is pretty good though.

But the premise underlying all that goofiness is something worthwhile. What is skateboarding all about? *Animal Chin* ends with an easy, tautological conclusion: "As long as skaters keep searching for Chin, they've already found him." Skating isn't about answers or endings; it's about the pursuit. Searching for Animal Chin led the crew to meet lots of people, skate some amazing spots, and, most importantly, to have fun, which is as close as the film is willing to get to providing an answer.

But what if one went about the search in a different way. Instead of looking for some anachronistic symbol of Eastern wisdom, what if I sought out meaning in the lives and accomplishments of people intimately involved in skateboarding? And what if instead of hoping for a single answer, I allowed for many? Skateboarding has so many facets—tricks, videos, culture, contests, industry—what if exploring them yielded something richer and more varied than mere fun? And what if skateboarding can speak to larger issues that go beyond itself? What if skateboarding can productively address bigger-picture topics like art and gender and economics and race? And what if everything we find isn't positive? What if searching for meaning pointed to ways to improve? And what if the culprits weren't some corporate suits, but ourselves?

Ever since that Christmas morning in 1995, I have seen skateboarding go through a lot of changes, just as I myself have grown and evolved. It has been so many different things for me—fun, exercise, camaraderie, anti-depressant, distraction, challenge, self-identity—that I have to allow that it's just as meaningful and versatile to others. As a portrait of skateboarding, this book is necessarily incomplete, but that is fitting, as one of the things that *Animal Chin* got right is that being a skateboarder, like being an artist, means never, ever being finished. You just keep pushing.

1 SINCE DAY ONE

"What's this? Some new kind of dance? No, it's America's newest sport, and it's called skateboarding." So begins a 1964 short film made by Bruce Brown, accompanied by footage of some bare-footed young boys in striped shirts basically kick-turning in circles in an anonymous lot. The boards are thin, free of grip tape, and flat as a plank. The wheels are clay, and the maneuverability is limited. For an ad featuring the Hobie Super Surfer Skateboard Team, the skaters don't exactly scream "super." They don't do much at all. They can't, really. Skateboarding had yet to progress into something more than mere novelty. In 1964, skateboards were toys. The kids on the Hobie team (who were among the best skaters at the time) look like beginners today—like, just-started-skating-a-month-ago beginners.

Although skateboarding didn't begin that year, it is the moment it became an industry. Before items like the Roller Derby Skateboard appeared on the market in 1959 and before Larry Stevenson published *The Quarterly Skateboarder* magazine, early iterations of the skateboard existed in various forms in various places since the beginning of the twentieth century. Many came from scooters with the handles removed, while others were made by attaching roller skates to two-by-fours. The actual "first" skateboard will never be correctly identified. Other books like Iain Borden's *Skateboarding and the City: A Complete History* (2019), Cole Louison's *The Impossible: Rodney Mullen, Ryan Sheckler, and the Fantastic History of Skateboarding* (2011), and Michael Brooke's *The Concrete Wave: The History of Skateboarding* (1999) have grappled with skating's murky origins, and I'm not going to add anything new to this conversation, at least in terms of historical documentation.

What interests me is the development of the culture of skateboarding, which only began to form in earnest once all the elements were in place. One of the most influential aspects of skateboarding was established in these initial boom years: danger. "From the very first moment that skateboarding hit the mainstream," Mark Waters told me, "the *Life* magazine cover. What does the caption say?" In May 1965 *Life* featured Patti McGee on its cover doing a handstand on a skateboard. McGee was one of the first professional skaters and one of its first champions. For a sport that, as we'll see, has been slow to embrace women, it's ironic that its first representative was not a man. The caption on the cover reads: "The Craze and the Menace of Skateboards." "And that was the first impression of skateboarders on a large scale," Waters continues. "The most popular magazine in the world at the time, to a large-scale audience. The *menace* of skateboards. So when we talk about progression in the mainstream, we started negative."

When I began to write this book, Waters was the first person I spoke to. Waters was involved in the skateboarding industry for over thirty years, and he'd skated long before that. He was a fountain of knowledge. I initially found Waters through the Skateboarding Hall of Fame in California, for which he served on the board of directors. We spoke over Zoom numerous times over a period of seven or eight months.

The "craze" of skating in the 60s was short-lived, sure, but at its peak, sales exploded. According to Cole Louison, "during a three-year period in the 1960s, a reported 50 million skateboards were made in America." Besides the cover of *Life*, skateboarders appeared on Johnny Carson's *The Tonight Show*, ABC's *Wide World of Sports*, a commercial for Kellogg's cereal, in magazines like *Newsweek* and *Popular Mechanics*, and even *The Wall Street Journal*. There was even a fucking pop song called "Sidewalk Surfin'" by Jan & Dean that reached number 25 on the Billboard Hot 100: "Grab your board and go sidewalk surfin' with me. / Don't be afraid to try the newest sport around. /Bust your buns, bust your buns now. / It's catchin' on in every city and town."

But the "menace" won out in the end, which came quickly and abruptly in 1966. The California Medical Association described skateboarding as "a new medical menace," echoing *Life*'s terminology. Skateboard sales plummeted. Cities banned skaters from public property. Moreover, the technology was there for skating to flourish. The limited maneuverability of the trucks, the clay wheels, the narrow decks—a couple of years was all you could get out of such a rudimentary device. Thus, the first impressions mainstream America had of skateboarding were perfectly captured by that *Life* cover. It was a dangerous fad.

When skateboarding returned to cultural relevance in the 1970s, it's no surprise that it was accompanied by major strides in the development of the gear, as well as a shift in culture. The introduction of urethane wheels by Frank Nasworthy's Cadillac Wheels and better truck design by companies like Independent gave skateboarding a brand-new life. From 1973 to 1980, a skater could choose from numerous sizes, weights, materials, and aesthetics. Skateboarding began to diversify technologically. The political landscape of the era— governmental distrust, anti-authoritarianism, iconoclasm— was also ripe for something like skateboarding, which was individualistic and rebellious.

Another new and important facet emerged: skateparks. The first one opened in Port Orange, Florida in 1976, with hundreds of other parks following. Not only did these vistas of rolling concrete engender new types of skating like bowl, vert, and park, it also provided skaters with a common ground, a place where they could congregate and form a community. Unfortunately, the parks were a little too popular. Insurance rates dumped on the park owners were unmanageable, despite the paucity of actual lawsuits.

This element of skate culture fascinates me, as it shows how much skateboarding can be influenced by forces outside of its immediate purview. Mark Waters clued me into this legal saga, which went beyond insurance policies. "Around the same time," Waters told me, "late-early 70s, say '73, that the Consumer Attorneys Association, a trade organization for consumer and trial lawyers said, 'We are running out of activities that we can take to court because of the hazardous recreational activities list.'"

The Hazardous Recreational Activity list is a set of risky activities that fall under the common law assumption of risk doctrine, which is a defense used in lawsuits that puts the blame for an injury on the injured party because they knew the risks involved in what they were doing. A municipality will designate certain things as "hazardous" to prevent people from suing cities (or making insurance claims). During this second wave of popularity, skateboarding wasn't on that list, and these lawyers had every incentive to keep it off that list, which meant that it was a liability, which meant that insurance rates were exorbitant, which meant that skateparks closed. As Waters wonderfully put it, "What happened is all around the country when the skate parks closed, there were all these kids that said, I'd like to skateboard, but I skateboard at the skateboard park, and the skateboard park's gone. I guess I don't skateboard anymore."

In the 1970s, lawsuits proliferated. The trampoline, for instance, led to thousands of injuries and endless litigation. Skateboarding—which, contrary to the language of *Life*, isn't actually that dangerous, studies have shown—was a victim of these circumstances. A *New York Times* piece in 1998 reported that "of the 200 parks built [in 1976], only 2 remain, most closed due to the threat of injury lawsuits." 198 skateparks closed because of an imagined threat. Skateboarding once again sank in popularity in the 80s, even though its culture continued to evolve and expand, cementing its foundations for future generations.

But we'll get to that period in a moment. First, I want to discuss what happened when skateboarding was finally added to the hazardous activities list. It happened in California in 1998. Despite mass closures of skate parks, skateboarding once again began to grow in the 90s. In an effort to stop kids from filling the streets (because, without parks, where the hell else were they going to go?), the courts realized—partly because the skate industry lobbied for it—that spaces needed to be created for them. Hence the passing of Health & Safety Code §115800, which declared, "Skateboarding in any facility or park owned or operated by a public entity as a public skateboard park, as provided in paragraph (3), shall be deemed a hazardous recreational activity within the meaning of §831.7 of the Government Code." §831.7 is the section covering liability in terms of hazardous recreational activities.

David Amell, in his academic article "F@#%K Pads: The Assumption of Risk Doctrine, Liability Limiting Statutes, and Skateboarding," he notes that while §115800 functioned as a "catalyst that started [a] chain reaction" for skateparks around the country, it also included a provision which forced "cities with skateparks to adopt ordinances requiring all skaters to wear kneepads, elbow pads and helmets." This might seem a reasonable request for the safety of skaters, but it actually left municipalities just as open to litigation as they had been before the code was passed. Here's why. Amell cites a "general rule of tort law," which states that everyone should exercise ordinary care and that each person "is liable for injuries caused by his [or her] failure to exercise reasonable care in the circumstances." However, as Amell puts it, "[t]his duty of care may be limited by the assumption of risk doctrine," which goes like this in the legislation: "A plaintiff who voluntarily assumes a risk of harm arising from the negligent or reckless conduct of the defendant cannot recover for such harm." "Recover" here means to be awarded recompense in a lawsuit. In subsequent cases regarding the assumption of risk doctrine, California courts further declared that "defendants have no legal duty to eliminate or decrease risks inherent in the sport" and that the "defendant's duty is limited to a duty not to increase the inherent risks."

So if a city builds a public park, all they are required to do under common law duty and the assumption of risk doctrine, is maintain the ramps and obstacles so that any damage to them doesn't increase the risks. They are not required to do anything additional. But, since §115800 essentially named a specific duty for cities to require safety gear, according to Amell, it "opened a door for plaintiffs that was closed under the common law."

A non-skater can be forgiven for believing that skateboarding is super dangerous, but studies show that it isn't any more perilous than more common sports like soccer and basketball, which in addition to being physically demanding activities also feature antagonistic opponents. The Consumer Product Safety Commission maintains a database called the National Electronic Injury Surveillance System (NEISS), which itemizes the number of injuries associated with sports and other recreational activities. For some reason, it groups skateboarding with scooters and hoverboards. In 2020 (a very popular year for skateboarding), the number of injuries for this grouping was 217,646. A large percentage of these are wrist-related, often sprains or fractures. There are an estimated 6.6 million skaters in the US and a whopping 85 million worldwide. According to one study, approximately 3% of skateboard-related injuries result in hospitalization. Of the 217,646, then, only 6,529 result in anything more serious than a visit to an ER. Remember, too, that this grouping includes two additional activities. In 2013, for instance, more than 4 million kids rode freestyle scooters, which have grown only more popular in the intervening years. And the same study cited above estimated that hoverboards sent 27,000 kids to the hospital between 2015 and 2016. Skateboarding, then, must only account for a much smaller percentage of those injuries. Let's say that skateboarding in 2020 caused 150,000 injuries (though the actual figure is likely fewer). The injury rate would be 2.3%; the number of hospitalizations would be 4,500.

All of which is to say that the statistics don't support the lingering characterization of skateboarding as reckless and dangerous. It isn't any more dangerous than the publicly funded team sports America celebrates so fervidly. Even though the world has in the past few decades accepted skateboarding as a legitimate part of culture, the fixation on safety still reigns. During the Olympics, Twitter users who were exposed to skating for the first time commented en masse that these skaters should be wearing helmets and pads. This is a sticking point for a lot of non-skaters, though it's also something that's slowly changing. For most of its history, street skaters didn't wear pads and would steadfastly refuse to if asked. It just wasn't something they did. Helmets, especially, intruded on skaters' vision, their comfort, and their balance. Vert skaters, however, always wore them, because the speeds and heights on those ramps reached fatal levels. Street skating, on the other hand, rarely does. Plus, there is a kind of machismo that a lot of skaters possess, dismissing the idea of pads because they're so tough and badass. Skating causes a lot of pain, and skaters pride themselves on their ability to handle it. There are memes all over social media contrasting skate injuries with, say, soccer injuries. Personally, I've bled from my elbows, knees, ankles, wrist, back, face, and hands more times than I can count. And I rarely missed school or work because of it. Skaters assume the doctrine of risk, not just in legal terms.

But perhaps you're saying to yourself, *Yeah, sure, helmets and safety aren't a part of the skater's ideology, but that's a stupid reason to maintain that future skaters shouldn't wear pads. Protection is more important than macho obstinance.* A pro skater like Andy Anderson wears a helmet on the streets, always, and his helmet isn't the same design as the clunkier bike helmets of the past. It's more like a baseball style one mixed with an Army cap. It clearly doesn't affect Anderson's abilities, as he's one of the most gifted riders out there. So maybe it's all posturing and retrograde chest-puffing. Maybe the claim that helmets are uncomfortable and get in the way are comparable to anti-mask people who get so bent out of shape about wearing a small piece of cloth over their faces while they shop at Target. Maybe we all need to evolve. Despite knowing this, I will never voluntarily wear a helmet when I skate. That's probably fucking idiotic of me, but it's the truth. Future generations will probably be smarter.

Mark Waters was involved in the campaign to get skateboarding added to the hazardous recreational activities list, which only partly explained his enthusiasm for the subject. But he didn't bring it up to boast. Waters was a lot of things— loquacious, a tad gossipy—but he was not arrogant. If anything, he was too self-effacing about his achievements.

For instance, I brought up Kyle Walker's "No Other Way" video part to Waters. (A video part is akin to a skater's highlight reel, a short compilation of their best tricks, filmed over the span of months or years. More on them in Chapter 3.) I will never forget the first time I saw it, as it shifted my perception about the behavior of skaters. It opens with a clip of Walker doing a back-tail kickflip out at MACBA, an infamous plaza in Barcelona that is daily overrun by skateboarders. When he lands, Walker turns to the camera with a big, shit-eating grin on his face, walks over, holds his shirt out so we can see the logo and says, "That's for y'all. That's for y'all." Throughout the rest of the part, his reactions to landing some of his tricks are not like those of other skaters. Sure, skaters will celebrate finally getting a scary or difficult trick (see, e.g., Chris Joslin take his shirt off after sticking something down a big stair set), but Walker's celebrations didn't seem to be of the thank-god-I-finally landed-it variety. They seemed, instead, like arrogance. After frontside flipping down a nine-stair plus a sidewalk, he narrowly avoids running into a curb. Then, he points to it and says, "That's what I wanted!" Rolling away from a back-smith grind down a handrail in San Francisco, Walker nods in a way that communicates something to the effect of: "Fuck yeah, I knew I had that shit." He does this thing, too, where he salutes someone off camera—presumably a friend who provided encouragement or who bet that he'd land this next attempt. He just has this attitude that you don't normally see in a skater's video part. The typical, I've-finally-landed-it, board-throwing exultation is a far cry from Walker's smug certainty.

But here's the thing: I fucking *love* this video part, and I love watching Walker skate. After a viewing or two, "No Other Way" shot up pretty high on my all-time favorites list. First of all, there's the music: Righteous Brothers' "Unchained Melody," which is itself a confident song choice and also one that works really well, despite its slow, romantic pace. But more than that, it's Walker's attitude. I came not only to accept his self-satisfied approach but also to embrace it.

Why *shouldn't* he be totally fucking stoked about what he'd just accomplished? Many of the tricks in his part are tricks that only a tiny, tiny fraction of skateboarders can perform—and many of the ones that can do them couldn't do them as beautifully as Walker does them. Dude has every right to be stoked on himself.

Here's what Waters said that prompted me to bring up Kyle Walker: "To me, when you learn a trick, it's your friends' job and place to cheer you for what you've accomplished. To me, that's a skateboarding thing. And the last thing I would ever do, like on Instagram or something—like even talking about this, I mean—even saying, like, Oh, I shot Eric [Koston]'s first photo, like, I'm even a little—it's not that I'm embarrassed that I did it, I'm a little embarrassed to point it out, or to say these things. And I don't know how to explain what that is. But it's the same mentality that I've had my whole life that came from skateboarding, that came from etiquette that I learned at the skate park and then learned the backyard ramp."

Let's unpack this a bit. For starters, I want to present a broader context for what Waters was saying here. Here is a condensed version of his resume. Waters really did shoot the first photo of Eric Koston to appear in a magazine. In the late 80s and early 90s, he shot photos of numerous luminaries and innovators, including Christian Hosoi, Jeff Grosso, Lance Mountain, Tom Knox, Ocean Howell, Mike Smith, Tommy Guerrero, Mike McGill, Lester Kasai, Alphonso Rawls, Damon Byrd, Mike Frazier, Dave Swift (one of skateboarding's most iconic photographers himself), and Tim Brauch, to name only a few, and published them in zines and skate mags. He worked at *Transworld* magazine and toured the country taking photos and writing articles, including one where he visited every skatepark in the US at the time (there were only around 45 in 1989!). In 1993, Waters joined Tum Yeto, the Tod Swank-founded company that ran Toy Machine, Foundation, and Pig Wheels, later adding Habitat, Ruckus, and Dekline. (The creation of the name Tum Yeto, for which Waters was present, came about because they tried to figure out a name that could be spelled out of the phone number they'd been assigned, 800-886-9386, so they could say, "Call 1-800-TUM-YETO for all your skateboard needs.") In 1998 Waters left the skate industry to work as a sound tech in film and television. His work with Tum Yeto was rewarding but not nearly as lucrative as a gig in the movie industry.

As a salute to Waters's work for the company, Toy Machine owner Ed Templeton included a shout out to Waters in one of their ads. It's an ad featuring an image of team rider Chris Senn mid-trick cut and pasted onto a photo of skyscrapers, as if he's skating on the buildings. In the corner of the page, there's a picture of Waters and a note: "this ad is dedicated to mark o. waters tum yeto employee 1993-1998." When I was a kid, Toy Machine was my favorite skate company, and I put every ad of theirs on my wall in rows. I had this same Toy Machine ad with Chris Senn and Mark Waters on my wall as a kid! When I figured this out, it totally blew my mind.

Unbeknownst to me, a photo of the guy I was interviewing hung over my dresser when I was a teenager. Such a wild and wonderful coincidence.

But it's also not all that surprising, because Waters has been involved in so many parts of skateboarding, his contributions so widespread, that inevitably something he worked on could be a part of a lot of skaters' childhoods. Younger skaters have a lot to thank Waters for. After his stint in the film industry, Waters returned to the skate world in the early 2000s, this time working for Sole Technology Inc. (usually referred to as Sole Tech), a shoe company that owns Etnies, Emerica, and éS brands. Through Sole Tech, Waters was instrumental in the creation of the éS Game of Skate, a tournament-style contest in which participants play a skateboard version of H.O.R.S.E. He was also part of the team, with Don Brown and Justin Regan and the International Association of Skateboard Companies (IASC), that implemented "Go Skateboarding Day" in 2004. Now named "Go Skate Day," the holiday is a mainstay in the skate community and celebrated every year on June 21. Over many years, Waters helped the petition to get skateboarding into the Olympics and served as the team's first head coach.

This is a hugely significant and influential skateboarding career. Not too many behind-the-scenes people have contributed as much to skateboarding as Mark Waters has. Dude was a major player. And yet he was reluctant to take credit for these things in a very public way. He would never, for instance, call out Steve Berra and his website, The Berrics, for borrowing the concept of a game of skate competition for their Battle at the Berrics, and even using some of the language Waters used in his original rules for éS Game of Skate. When Waters spoke to me of the Battle at the Berrics, he wasn't upset as much as he was a little disappointed. "I don't think they stole it," he said. "The way the Berrics did it, you know. I carry that a tiny, tiny bit. Some people would go, 'Why?' Because they honestly don't know. But those guys know." Despite his grievance, Waters would never make a big public fuss.

Waters attributes this trait—his unwillingness to stake claim for his achievements—to being a skateboarder, which is a fascinating claim, one that has some truth to it but is also a bit disingenuous. Waters was right that skaters aren't historically supposed to hype their own shit, but to me that's only a matter of posture. The truth is that skaters don't want to be seen hyping themselves up, because of course so much of skating is showing off. Skaters go on sessions with their friends and do the best tricks they can possibly do, or they do the ones that look the best. We go to skateparks and pull out our best lines. We feed on the energy of the crowd and suddenly try tricks we've never even done before. Video parts, contests, Instagram clips, magazine spreads—it's all a performance. No one skates purely for validation, but it certainly spurs us on. So, even though when we land a rad trick we aren't clapping for ourselves, we're just as much participants in the hype as the cheering audience. The phrase "video or it didn't happen" captures the skate ethos. Some kid talking about doing some crazy stuff without proof is taken about as seriously as a UFO sighting. Skateboarding is 10% aspiration, 20% perspiration, and 70% documentation. We don't skate in a vacuum.

Waters was born in 1966, so he was part of a different generation, one that experienced the ups and downs of the popularity of skateboarding throughout the 80s and 90s. Kyle Walker, on the other hand, was born in 1994, which means he never knew a time when skateboarding wasn't accepted by culture as legitimate. Perhaps the tenuous oscillation of the skate industry instilled into Waters' cohort a humbler attitude, as they never knew when it could all come crashing down again.

The way Waters saw it, each popularity peak of skateboarding introduced new "diehards" to the lifestyle, who stayed on beyond the next valley. "Looking at the diehards in '91 versus the diehards in '81 or '82—the number [in '91] was far greater." Those who skated in the 60s, 70s, and 80s because it was a fad would inevitably stop skating, but each wave brought on an admittedly much smaller number of committed rippers. After three waves of popularity (as Michael Brooke defines them in *The Concrete Wave*: first, 1959–65; second, 1973–80; and third, 1983–91), skating had amassed a core group, and it was this collection of dedicated skaters who progressed things when the casuals bailed, the corporate money dried up, and the sponsors dropped their teams. Each influx of cash and attention provided the true skaters with the means to develop and experiment. Demand yielded the new technologies of the 70s, and the competition circuit of the 80s (freestyle and vert) gave life to most of the tricks we know today. But once the funding disappeared, it was up to the skaters to push things along.

The end of the third wave in 1991 represents, I would argue, the most significant shift in skateboarding. The mass closure of skateparks forced the now sizable (but still relatively small) skate community into the streets, which is where it thrives most productively, because even when skateparks were popular, most people around the world didn't have access to them. A kid watching an 80s video filled with ramps and pools wouldn't be able to translate their stoke into action; a kid watching a video in the 90s, where most of the skating occurs in recognizable terrain, just like the kind right outside their window, could grab their board and attempt to replicate what they saw on screen. Street skating happened in the 80s, of course, with skaters like Natas Kaupas spinning on fire hydrants in *Streets on Fire* and Tommy Guerrero shredding the streets in the Powell Peralta videos, but it truly came to life in the early 90s. Skateboarding is not unlike soccer, which is globally popular because it requires so little to play. All you need is a ball and some grass. To skate, you just need a skateboard and some concrete. The crash of the early 90s actually helped skateboarding grow in a larger sense: street skating exploded, so you no longer needed a skatepark to learn.

By the time that the X-Games launched in 1995—and particularly by the time the X-Games registered in the zeitgeist in '97 or '98,—street skating flourished, so anyone introduced to skating by these large-scale contests would discover troves of videos and magazines featuring Mike Carroll, Eric Koston, Stevie Williams, Guy Mariano, and numerous others just destroying ledges and stairs and picnic tables and banks. Even if you yearned to try out the ramps and obstacles featured in the X-Games, there was plenty of street footage to hype you up in the absence of a local park.

The business side of things, too, changed after the end of the second wave. "At this point," Waters told me, "the industry [was] starting to be self-sustaining and growing without worrying as much about those fad kids that would come in and leave." In the 80s, there was what Brooke refers to as a "Big Five" in skateboarding: Powell Peralta, Santa Cruz, Tracker, Independent, and Vision. (Editor and writer Mackenzie Eisenhour designates this a "Big Three," excluding Tracker and Independent from the list.) As Eisenhour puts it, these companies "held everything from Park Place to the Utility Companies on the Monopoly Board." That is, until smaller, skater-owned brands like Steve Rocco's World Industries (co-founded with Rodney Mullen) joined the fray and functioned a lot better during the economic downturn. Rocco practiced a shrewd and sometimes ethically questionable business style, but his innovative marketing proved successful. He understood the language of skaters better than larger companies, and his example created the template for how to run a skate company.

In 1999, Tony Hawk landed a 900 during the X-Games, and, as Waters put it, "ESPN decided to make that a much bigger deal than it was to skateboarding." For skaters, the clip of Hawk tirelessly going after that elusive trick—one that had haunted a number of vert skaters over the years, like Danny Way, who nearly landed one almost a decade earlier—would have become an iconic moment, certainly, the kind of highlight you rewatch occasionally in subsequent years. But ESPN's promotion of the 900 turned it into a cultural phenomenon. Any skater coming up during this period experienced comments from strangers who, upon seeing their skateboard, said some shit like, "Do a 900!"

Tony Hawk was already a well-known figure at that point, but the 900 (and the release just three months later of *Tony Hawk's Pro Skater* on Playstation) made him a household name. "The thing that changed in '99," Waters said, "when Tony did that, was the business. I mean, I know people started skateboarding more, but probably around 2015, there are probably around the same number of skateboarders that we were in 1999, before Tony Hawk did the 900, if that makes sense. Because what we gained from '99 to 2008—a significant number of those fell off in 2008 again. So, it's just a series of peaks and valleys that affect business but also affect overall numbers."

Skateboarding began as a "menace," a dangerous activity rife with potential litigation. Tony Hawk's rise to fame played a large role in changing that perception. Consider that only four years earlier Larry Clark's film *Kids*, written by Harmony Korine, hit theaters and characterized skaters as violent druggie rapists. Hawk is about as far as you can get away from

Kids while still remaining on the same planet. Hawk came of age in the 80s with the Bones Brigade, a team of skaters put together by Stacy Peralta, a former pro turned businessman and eventual filmmaker (he directed the documentaries *Bones Brigade: An Autobiography* and *Dogtown & Z Boys,* and wrote the screenplay for the film adaptation *Lords of Dogtown*, starring Emile Hirsch and Heath Ledger). The Bones Brigade were a pretty clean-cut group of kids: they didn't drink or do drugs, didn't cause chaos on their tours. Hawk, then, represented a swift contradiction to the "menace" mainstream culture believed skateboarding to be.

During this post-900 era, Waters worked for Sole Tech and became involved in the process of getting skateboarding into the Olympics. "Basic economics," Waters explained, "created the desire. And by that I mean the Olympics has, over many years, slowly become an older person's television show." In a report published in *Communication & Sport*, authors Belinda Wheaton and Holly Thorpe note that, "The median age of U.S. viewers for the 2008 Beijing Olympics was 47, rising to 48 for the 2012 London Games, and 53 for the 2016 Rio Games." In 1998, the Olympics added snowboarding to the slate of events. The president of the International Olympic Committee at the time, Jacques Rogge, explained that the addition was "to spark popularity with young people," a feat snowboarding accomplished. Snowboarding had a slightly easier road to the Olympics, since they could simply fall under the governorship of the International Ski Federation (even though snowboarders would have much preferred the

International Snowboard Federation). In order for a sport to join the Olympics, it has to have a global governing body.

Since skiing has been established for decades, it had such an entity that snowboarding could be subsumed into. Skateboarding, on the other hand, had competing organizations in various states of disorder. "So at some point after Salt Lake City," Waters said, "there was a general awareness that skateboarding was being considered, and this is coming from the Olympics, you know, NBC, whoever. The way I heard it was that they said, you know, we want skateboarding to do for the Summer Olympics, what snowboarding has helped do for the Winter Olympics." So, Waters and a handful of others—including Tony Hawk, pro skater Andy MacDonald, IASC founder Jim Fitzpatrick, Tum Yeto founder Tod Swank, and Don Bostick, the owner of World Cup Skateboarding—got together to assess the situation. Their goal was not to get skateboarding into the Olympics, but rather, "only to ensure that if skateboarding was going to enter into the Olympics, that it would be done with as much influence from actual skateboarders and skaters and people who represented skateboarding and had skateboarding's long-term best interests at heart to chaperone it into the Olympics."

Then in 2004 in Münster, Germany, at the Münster Monster Mastership contest, another meeting was held, this one featuring people from many countries around the world—"what would become ISF, the International Skateboarding Federation"—to figure out the logistics of establishing a global entity to represent skateboarding and then to create relationships with skating organizations on the national level. At the end of the meeting, they voted to form ISF. There was a hiccup, though. An international governing body that was recognized by the IOC already existed and claimed skateboarding under its umbrella. The Fédération Internationale de Roller Sports (FIRS) was founded in 1924 by Fred Renkewitz and Otto Myer, and it put on contests for inline speed skating and roller hockey. The ISF was therefore in competition with FIRS. Since the organization that would end up officially representing skateboarding to the IOC stood to make a lot of money, neither ISF nor FIRS was willing to step back.

It wasn't until 2017, nearly fifteen years later, that the two federations merged into a single one, now known as World Skate, which covers, in addition to skateboarding, inline alpine, inline downhill, inline freestyle, inline hockey, rink hockey, roller derby, roller freestyle, scooter, and skate cross. This move may seem like it could have solved all of the problems, but it didn't. Waters had not too many nice things to say about World Skate, who he claimed repeatedly ignored the suggestions and input of USA Skateboarding, including those of Josh Friedberg, who before becoming the CEO of USA Skateboarding was the Skateboarding Director at World Skate. "These are people," Waters said, "who are, in my estimation, out for power and the eventual money that will come once skateboarding is an official sport in the Olympics." (Skateboarding, of course, participated in the 2020 Olympics in Tokyo, but it still wasn't an "official" Olympic sport. It was a host city sport, which limits the funding and the profit share from the broadcast, which is to say: skateboarding gets none of it.) Waters continued: "These guys are running what in my experience were the worst skateboarding events that we've had since the 90s. And they don't accept help. And they don't have the same experience working with skateboarders that a lot of people do."

Skateboarding, along with another new addition, surfing, did boost the ratings at the Tokyo Olympics, and it's been officially approved for the games in Paris in 2024. Hopefully World Skate gets their shit together, as they are now global stewards for something that for so long resisted organizational officialdom. Entire generations of kids will first learn about skateboarding through the Olympics and the events World Skate puts on. World Skate will therefore play a major role in how future skaters go into it—and what they'll believe skating is all about. They have a responsibility to the beauty and radness of skateboarding to maintain as much of its true spirit as possible, or at least allow for multiplicity within its borders.

The skateboard is a child of land and sea. Its hybrid origins are fitting, as its history is one of multi-faceted influences and cultural cross pollination. The aesthetic of skateboarding has gone from surfer-adjacent to many iterations in punk, hardcore, and hip hop, the latter of which probably had the biggest influence in the last few decades. It began as a toy and became an art form. It originated in the west coast of America and now has thriving communities in every country in the world. There is no longer a singular culture of skateboarding but rather cultures.

But all of those shifts also include its corporatization. Historically, skaters were anti-corporation. Think back to that opening scene of *Animal Chin*, where Stacy Peralta chucks his TV out the window because he so objects to the businessman espousing his financial definition of skateboarding. Since 2000, the skate industry has seen the entrance of Nike, Adidas, New Balance, Monster Energy, Redbull, and numerous other corporate juggernauts into the scene. There was some resistance to these brands cashing in without earning their stripes, but the money they introduced proved too valuable to skaters who had for a long time survived on a few hundred bucks a month from sponsors. Professional skaters got a taste of what other professional athletes have always had: they not only get a better salary, they have access to high-quality training facilities, trainers, doctors, rehab specialists. The problem with a small-scale industry was that skaters were never adequately compensated. Many still aren't, but more are now than ever before.

Waters, though, worries about what will happen in the future, if skateboarding will go through another one of its valleys. "I've given up some of my idealism," he said. "And I'll be honest, if I had been independently wealthy, I never would have, but I've given up some ideals for practicality's sake, in my personal life. But here's the bottom line: if skateboarding went away, Nike, Adidas, New Balance, probably Element, probably Volcom—all these publicly traded companies? Bye bye. They're not going to be in skateboarding. Nike's gonna go back to, you know, an emphasis on tennis shoes that look good."

Because of the Olympics, skating will continue to be profitable for at least the next five to ten years, but Waters' pessimism is well founded. Millions were made in the 60s and 80s before things went belly-up. Who's to say that there won't be another crash in popularity? And when those companies pull out, what state will they leave skateboarding in?

The future is, of course, uncertain, a fact that is tragically emphasized by the conversations I had with Waters. As I mentioned, he was the original head coach for the US Olympic men's team. At some point, however, he vacated that position. When I asked him why, he said, "I'm not trying to be mysterious, but it's just not something I want to air." He made a "30-second mistake" and dismissed the whole situation as "really fucking stupid." Whatever happened clearly left him regretful, upset, and "bummed." But then he said: "It's something that, you know, I'm probably going to struggle with during the Olympics next year."

This conversation took place in November 2020. The Olympics finally took place in July and August 2021, a mere eight months later. Waters didn't get to watch the Olympics and struggle with his feelings about them because he tragically died in January from COVID. He never got to see what he'd helped make happen. More importantly, he won't get to see his son grow up in a world that Waters made better through his time in it. Waters was a wonderful person, and in our nine conversations totaling more than 27 hours, he became a friend. He connected me with some of the people I interviewed here, and he provided me with invaluable resources to help me with this book. I cannot express how shocking and saddening it was to hear of his passing.

Mark Waters didn't celebrate himself; it wasn't in him to toot his own horn. "To me," he said, "when you learn a trick, it's your friends' job and place to cheer you for what you've accomplished." For what it's worth, I hope I've been able to do that for him. This is for Mark—a rousing, standing ovation for what he accomplished.

2 PHOTOSYNTHESIS

In the present moment, skateboarding lives on Instagram and YouTube and, more and more, on TikTok. Skaters and brands post clips every day, the mass of footage so vast it's overwhelming. And although there's an unspoken rule that you save your best shit for your video part, skaters still post some insane stuff. YouTube, on the other hand, is where the video parts go. Even if they begin life on another outlet (like, say, *Thrasher*'s website), they find their biggest audience on YouTube. Videos, in other words, dominate skateboarding.

But that wasn't always the case. For most of the first decades of skateboarding, photography ruled the day.

Photography in general used to be a legitimate, even lucrative career path. Jonathan Mehring, one of the top photographers in skateboarding, certainly believed this as a kid in the early 90s. "Newsstands used to be insane, like, options and everything. And it just seemed like, yeah, this is totally viable. I should try to focus on this. I didn't think about skating as a career path."

Mehring grew up in Virginia and though he didn't consider skating as a possible career, he was definitely a skater. In fact, he was in the much-coveted position of "the kid with the mini-ramp." Like its name suggests, a mini ramp is a small version of a vert ramp, ranging anywhere from three-feet to six feet or so high. Once you get bigger than six feet, the name mini becomes a misnomer. In the '90s, you could order mini ramp plans from *Thrasher*, something all skaters dreamed about. When I was a kid, I tried to get my parents to buy me the plans and build a ramp in my backyard. I truly thought it would be easy. My father disabused me of that notion swiftly.

But there was a kid in my town whose parents did build him a mini. His name was Jeff and he wasn't a skateboarder; he was a Rollerblader. (Rollerblade is technically the name of a company and not the term for the activity, but no one I've ever known as a kid or adult ever referred to it as "in-line skating.") I went over to Jeff's house a lot that first summer. Back then, there weren't many skateparks around, so getting to ride an actual ramp—the kind we saw in videos—was quite a thrill. However, despite the exposure, I never found my footing in transition skating.

Neither did Mehring. "I never got very good at skating" in general, he told me. For starters, his mini-ramp was shitty: fearing splinters, his dad put the grain of the wood perpendicular to the ramp instead of along the length of it, which makes it ride slow; not wanting to spending additional money on coping, Mehring's father cut PVC pipe in half and attached it to the top of each side, which is soft and grinds poorly. But more than that, his interest in photography superseded his passion for progressing as a skater.

A progressively apathetic high school student, Mehring's grades slipped every year until his parents suggested he take a photography class taught by one of their friends. Her name was Mrs. Roebuck. "She was actually super cool, and I went from getting Cs and Ds to, like, showing up an hour early for school to go to the darkroom. I got super into it. And so the obvious thing was to shoot my friends skating because I was already an avid skater at that point." This is a common occurrence: most skate photographers are skaters themselves, which is pretty much required so that they understand the nuances of the tricks they're capturing. You want to make sure that the angle you pick offers the best view of the trick, the skater, and the obstacle, so that everything is clear upon a single look. But you also want to make the trick look as gnarly as possible, so you can't just snap an image from straight on. Often the best angles are from low to the ground looking up at the skater as they fly past, which puts the photographer in a dangerous position—again another way that actually being a skater benefits anyone undertaking such a vocation: you've got to know when to get the fuck out of the way. Moreover, you're probably going to get hit by a board occasionally, and anyone who skates will be better equipped to deal with the pain.

"I guess that was my way to be part of the scene," Mehring said, "you know, the local scene. Not that I wasn't part of it, but that I could add value, I guess." And he's absolutely right.

Photographers—especially in the 90s—were and are a vital part of a skater's career. If you're adept with cameras, and if your photos get published in skate mags, you eventually will be in demand. And back then, in fact, "the photographer always got first choice of the spot to shoot from," Mehring said. "I guess it was the thinking that the filmer could move, right? But you know, I could always be like, 'Hey, sorry, filmer, you're in my shot.'"

When he was a senior, he bought a fisheye lens, a super wide-angle lens that at its most extreme makes the shot look like a reflection in a mirrored ball, like that M.C. Escher self-portrait, "Hand with Reflecting Sphere." For skate photographers, the purpose of fisheye is to makes tricks and spots look bigger. A simple flat-ground kickflip will appear twice as high as it really popped. Still images using fisheye don't use as much distortion as some video from the time. There are videos where you can see the edges of the lens and the terrain bends to the rim. It can be cartoonish and frustrating to watch.

Armed with gear and experience shooting skating, Mehring attended Virginia Commonwealth University where he earned a BFA in Photography. He also began submitting photos to skate magazines. His first publication was in *Thrasher* in March 2000, in a feature about a contest called "Beast of the East," which took place in Raleigh, North Carolina in December 1999. Mehring snapped a photo of, in his words, "Chris Cole doing a benihana to fakie on a quarter pipe with a helmet on." Any excitement Mehring might have had for his first published photo was soon deflated by the realities of the freelance existence:

> I got a little bit disillusioned because they took, like, months and months to pay me. I was calling the photo editor like every fucking day. Probably before they even had gone through to see who shot the photos and process the payments for the mag, you know. But months later he picked up the phone. I had gone down to once a week at that point. It was Luke Ogden. He picked up and I was like, Hey, it's Jonathan Mehring. I've been calling you. And he was like, Yeah, I know. Let me pay you.

I asked him how much they paid him for that first photo.

"It was $100."

Slap Magazine, however, turned out to be much more responsive to Mehring's submissions. After graduation, Mehring moved to DC and went on missions with his crew. "I had been focusing on shooting photos of my friends," he said, "and trying to get my friends in the mag, which had actually worked on one occasion." This occasion was his friend Will Lee backside tailsliding a ledge in Charlottesville. It was a two-page spread. "I was super stoked on that."

Then, Joe Brook—then-photographer and -editor for *Slap* at the time and long-time staff photographer for *Thrasher*—called Jonathan and said, "We like you. We want you to shoot for us. But can you shoot pros? We need you to shoot pros."

So Mehring put together an article on the DC scene called "The Forgotten City," featuring a bunch of his photos and writing. Brook and editor Mark Whiteley liked the piece and offered to put Mehring on retainer. The only caveat: he had to move to Philadelphia, where, they said, "the scene [was] popping off." Despite his reservations ("Philly had a reputation for being tough"), Mehring relocated to Pennsylvania for the opportunity. What he didn't know, however, was that he was replacing another photographer, whose retainer would go to Mehring as soon as he arrived. "This dude," he said, "his name was Frankie. Like, this guy fucking hates my guts. And I'm like, Why does this guy hate me so much? [Laughs.] Anyway, we clashed."

It turned out Philly was just as tough as he'd heard:

There were a lot of pros there. There were also a lot of photographers. And there weren't that many filmers. So there'd be large groups of skaters attached to each filmer and the photographers scurrying around with who they could for the day. It was a fucking feeding frenzy, man. Very, very, very competitive. It was super crazy. But then other visiting photographers would come into town and it was like people poaching each other's shit.

Skating in Philly from the 90s until the early 2000s centered around Love Park in Center City. The downtown plaza is technically called John F. Kennedy Plaza, but the iconic sculpture designed by Robert Indiana—the word LOVE in big red serif font arranged so that the L and the O sit on top of the V and E—gave the park its accepted moniker. Love Park featured a wide array of terrain that was ideal for skateboarding: smooth ground, ledges of varying sizes, stair sets (including an infamous four-block), benches, and gaps. Skaters like Stevie Williams and Josh Kalis exemplify the Love Park style. Williams did these impossibly long lines that included some crazy difficult tech tricks, a lot of which were switch, while Kalis manipulated the space like a kid playing with Legos. He'd stick a skateboard under one end of one of the granite tiles that made up the ground to create a ramp, and he would launch over trash cans. Or he'd put a plastic Jersey barrier down the stairs and grind it like a handrail. The park became a destination for skaters from all over the world. There are numerous clips of police chasing out huge crews of kids. The skaters were probably a nuisance to the city, but Love Park was home to a lot of young people who didn't have much else in their lives. Love Park gave them a family. The writer Maxwell Neely-Cohen described the spot's aura in a piece for *Buzzfeed* in 2016, after the park was completely redesigned with more green space:

> I experienced Love Park for the first time the same year I experienced the Roman Coliseum for the first time. Their impressions still reign equal in my memory. Architectural marvels given over to human spectacle. In Love I heard the same hushed reverence that always rang through my ears when I would walk into an old church. My atheist self

would take off my baseball cap out of respect, and listen to that dead noise. In between the pops and the grinds Love Park had that sound. Gravitas bouncing off of stone. Except I could keep my hat on.

If you think the idea of skaters having sacred spaces sounds absurd or silly, then you're underestimating the dexterity of reverence. Growing up I saw Love Park in dozens of skate videos until it seemed a fantasy place, a Hollywood set. When I saw it for the first time in person, I too felt a tinge of something close to holiness.

In 2003, there was an intensive crackdown on skating and loitering and homelessness in Love Park, effectively shutting it down as a spot. A lot of skaters were fined or even arrested. For Mehring, it seemed like a time to go. "Kalis moved away. A bunch of people moved out west. I was like, You know what? I'm going to New York. This is my moment." Only a few years out of college, Mehring moved to his third city in as many years.

Slap offered Mehring the opportunity to travel with skate teams. His first trip was around the Eastern US, but he soon got the chance to go to Hong Kong for 411's video series *Around the World*. Joining him were pros Ricky Oyola, Damian Smith, Kenny Reed, and Cairo Foster. "I was super nervous," he said, "because it was Kenny and Cairo. I was like, Oh my god, these guys are big-time pros, you know? I've never been out of the country except I think I'd been to Mexico one time with my parents." The trip didn't go well. Mehring had "the cheapest gear ever," which included his radio transmitter for his flashes. Radio transmitters allow photographers to trigger their flashes wirelessly. But Hong Kong proved to be an arduous place for a neophyte cameraman. The city "was so much more technologically advanced that there were all kinds of more radio frequencies going on and they were interfering with my cheapo stuff. What happened is that I would plug them in, and they would start making my flash pop, pop, pop, pop, pop, pop, pop, pop, pop, until it would kill the battery."

He missed numerous photos, mostly of Foster. "But they always seemed to work for Kenny, for some reason. So that helped make a wonderful relationship with Kenny. But I didn't talk to Cairo for a number of years after that. So that really sucked."

The photography program at Virginia Commonwealth University didn't equip him with adequate knowledge to avoid some of these mishaps. "It was run by a bunch of photographers," he recalled, "who worked in the local market in Virginia, and they all had aspirations to be, like, big commercial photographers or whatever, but none of them actually were. So they would push this vision onto you but not be able to actually tell you how to get there." And they were discouraging of his work in the skate world—not that he needed help with that. "My photography education kind of suffered because of that. I could definitely shoot a trick, like, very well. The rest was lacking. I had to figure that shit out on my own, basically, and it took a long time."

After the Hong Kong article, a substantial piece for Mehring, was published in *Slap* he toured Europe with the Zoo York team for a month. Even in these initial novice learning experiences, Mehring began to realize how much he wanted to explore the world as much as he could. Moreover, he longed to travel to locales not typically associated with skateboarding, places to which, perhaps, no skater had ever been.

Here's how Jonathan Mehring organized his skate trips:

Basically, these companies pay for ads—ad space in the magazines. And then in exchange, the magazines run photos of their guys on a strictly business base level. So it used to be this kind of symbiotic relationship where the advertisers would pay for the magazine and the magazine would pay them back with editorial content. So the easiest way, the most efficient way to get that would be to get the whole team together and go on a trip somewhere, so everyone's very focused on their task at hand getting tricks. And then there was kind of this unwritten rule that the footage would always—the videos would come out much later than the magazines. So all the photos would come out as kind of like a preview of what was going to be in an upcoming video. And if you were on it, you would collect all the magazines, you'd see all the different tours of all the same teams and be like, okay, so like, yeah, and people would tally the tricks and make sure they're in the video and what wasn't getting landed and all that.

When I was a kid, I never gave a second thought to the logistics of the skate trips covered in skate mags. Hearing Mehring describe this "symbiotic relationship," it makes sense things were done this way. Videos were much rarer in the 90s and early 2000s—a glimpse of their content in magazine features sated one's eagerness.

Skate trips are a major part of the skateboarding industry. Teams use them to film videos and shoot photos for magazine spreads, but they also do demos at local skateparks, where locals stand around the perimeter and watch their favorite skaters rip familiar terrain. I can't emphasize enough how much seeing a pro skate your skate park changes your perspective of what can be done there. A pro skater—especially one with a crowd—will do tricks that you never accomplished in all your years as a local. It's humbling and inspiring. But sometimes a local kid won't be able to simply stand back and watch their park get destroyed by outsiders, pro or not. And thus, the legend of the hometown hero was born.

A hometown hero is a ripper, a greatly talented skater who, to the rest of the community, is viewed in a similar way that pros are to the wider culture. At their local spot, they dominate. In my experience, these kids aren't always the most approachable. I often see them wearing earbuds, the music separating them from the world around them. They don't talk when they're in the zone; they just tear around the park doing rad shit. But when a skate team rolls into town, a heightened sense of territoriality comes over the hometown hero, and they must defend their turf, show off for the celebrities, try to make an impression, and maybe—just maybe—nudge forward their skate career.

Pros must hate these kids. In a 1999 tour article for *Transworld*, titled "Hometown Hero Versus Toy Machine," Ed Templeton defines the term as "a local ripper who comes to the demo and tries really hard to 'one up' the visiting team. The crowd always cheers for him the most." Now, Templeton makes a point of saying that his piece isn't "a condemnation of hometown heroes. If I was a good unsponsored skater, and a team came to my local spot, I would rip it up also," but how irksome must the following moment have been?

> We headed for downtown Tulsa to skate a local spot. All the kids from the demo were there waiting for us. There was a small rail they wanted us to skate. Brian [Anderson] and I didn't feel like skating the rail, but the kids started talking shit, so we skated it to satisfy them. I asked what had been done on the rail, and this kid gave me an immediate list: "Five-O, tailfakie, lip, lipfakie, frontboard all done by me." Then the Hometown Hero pulled out all of his moves and his pals cheered him on. One kid said out loud, "Tulsa, five points. Toy Machine, one point." We thought skating the rail would stoke the kids out, but obviously we were lured into a contest.

I mean, I can't imagine what it must be like to be a pro, with kids constantly trying to impress you or ask you to do certain tricks or begging for free shit. To a certain degree, they must get used to this kind of thing, so perhaps hometown heroes aren't as annoying as they seem. But this is what pros have to deal with on tours. Mehring, as a photographer, dealt with very different obstacles. Namely, the logistics.

(While reading the "Hometown Hero Versus Toy Machine" article for this chapter, which I had read as a fourteen-year-old and remembered to this day, I came across this passage in it: "Out of nowhere, Mark Waters, our old team manager, called Bam's cell phone and said he was in Lawrence [Kansas] waiting for us. We met him at a hotel and spent the night hanging out with Mark and his two dogs." It shook me to see Mark just pop up in this, but, just like the Toy Machine ad he was in, Mark's fingerprints were all over skateboarding and my childhood. The next day, Templeton writes, "It was fun seeing Mark again and strange seeing him in Kansas of all places." This was how I felt when I read his name. It was good seeing Mark again.)

On those early tours with *Slap*, Mehring not only dealt with the logistics—which involved coordinating with team managers and editors and skaters and various practicalities like flights, van rentals, filmers, and gear—but he also had to earn the respect of the skaters. By the time a skater becomes pro, they usually have one or two photographers who they exclusively work with, so if you're an up-and-comer it's hard to break into the game. And Mehring, in these early days, had few connections.

"That's why I feel it was so hard," he said, "because I literally did not know anyone. And at first, the only guys who would shoot with me were the guys who were sponsored, kind of, but they"re trying to get sponsored, or they"re trying to get pro. Like, the Maldonado's and the Kerry Getz's didn't really show me the time of day."

Until, that is, Mehring got a cover shot. An image of Josh Kalis kickflipping over a trash can in Love Park appeared on the cover of *Slap* in February 2000, and "after that, all of a sudden everyone's like, Oh, yeah, let's go." Entry into skate photography, like any competitive industry, revolves around one of those almost tautological catch-22s: "You couldn't shoot with the pros unless you shot with the pros." But now Mehring could shoot with the pros because he shot with the pros . . . and he could get them on covers.

Although *Slap* gave Mehring his introduction into the skate scene and allowed him to travel to fascinating locales like Hong Kong, they didn't pay him well. In fact, Mehring felt "nickel and dimed" by *Slap*. "I was getting burnt out," he said, "and I was making zero money. Like really struggling to live. I was working and really not getting paid a living wage. I was just like, Fuck, man. This is brutal." Plus, those early trips instilled into Mehring a desire to seek out more and more exotic places, countries and cities skaters rarely—or never—visited. But he wanted to be in charge, to organize the operation and handpick the skaters. "My thing is I was always all about bringing my friends and getting them in the magazine," he said. He wanted to be the director of the tour. And that wasn't going to happen at *Slap*.

A shakeup at *Skateboarder* gave him the perfect opportunity to defect from *Slap* and move on. They offered him double what he was making at *Slap* (which was a paltry $750 a month), and plus, his mind was set on unique skate trips:

> And the first thing I did was like, 'Hey, I want to take like a random crew of dudes.' I called around to sponsors. I didn't really understand the standard business model. I didn't really care to, I guess, at that time. But I was just like, these guys all rip. I'd hit up each team manager and be like, 'Hey, I want to do this trip for *Skateboarder*. Can you just give me like a little money to cover this guy's expenses? Like, it's gonna be like 2500 bucks.'

The prospect of getting one of their skaters in the mag usually led companies to pay for their rider's expenses. But one expense always proved problematic: the filmer. "It was always a challenge to get the filmer paid for," Mehring explained. "Because they were like this excess person. They didn't work for any of the brands. Or maybe the filmer worked for one of the companies, but then they're like, 'we don't want our guys giving footage to a competitor.'" Though he often managed to get someone to cover the filmer, "out of every trip that happened, there was probably two or three that didn't because of that."

For *Skateboarder*, Mehring travelled a lot, but he was regularly tasked with more standard fare like team demo tours. Still, he constantly pitched his own ideas. A bit of serendipity created what he became one of the first trips that satisfied his particular itch. "I was talking to Kenny Reed. And he was in Russia on this Planet Earth trip. He was like, 'It ends on this date, but I have a visa that extends to a longer date. Do you want to bring some guys out to Moscow and we'll just skate around? We can go to Latvia, Lithuania, Bulgaria.' Like, Bulgaria was kind of a hotspot, weirdly." So Mehring brought Jack Sabback and Bobby Puleo along to meet up with Kenny. Since they all rode for iPath Footwear, Mehring got the shoe and apparel brand to pay for the filmer.

The trip featured the chaos typical for such a journey. For example, Mehring and crew got kicked out of the apartment Kenny Reed had rented because they had eleven guys crashing there. It was 11:30 at night. They ended up staying at a local photographer's place. "It's like in this sketchy old building on the outskirts of town, you know, and it's super grimy. And like, we go in and there's not a single thing in the apartment—like, he's fully moved out. Like, not one piece of furniture. And then there's these blankets and pillows in this cupboard, up by the ceiling. And I just remember him putting them up there and shutting the door and saying, 'Those are my girlfriend's. You guys can't use them.'" It turned out the guy was in between apartments, and this was his previous one. "So he leaves and he's like, 'If anyone knocks on the door, don't answer it.'"

The Russia trip cost between six and seven grand. But Mehring's next idea would cost a good deal more than that. He wanted to take the Trans-Siberian Railway.

"I've never ever heard of the thing before," Mehring said of the longest railway in the world (over 5,700 miles). "And so I was like, Holy shit. That sounds amazing. So then all of 2006 I tried to get that going." The problem, again, was getting a filmer paid for. Plus, he travelled internationally multiple times a year for other assignments for *Skateboarder*, which meant that organizing a massive undertaking like the Trans-Siberian adventure had to be done on his own already-minimal time. But his time in Russia fueled a desire to go on more "adventure trips." "After that is when I was like, Man, I want to do more adventure trips. Like I said, before, I had kind of got burned out on just documenting tricks, and I wanted— I *needed* to find a way to see my own interest in what I was doing." His non-travel time wasn't exactly leisurely, as any time he was home in New York (where he'd moved in 2003), he embarked on missions with skaters. New York photographers like Giovanni Reda and Mike O'Meally inspired the relocation, in addition to the city's general appeal as a cultural epicenter.

The skate photography world being relatively small and very competitive, Mehring's friend and pro skater Pat Smith encouraged him to let New York photographers like Reda know ahead of time that he was moving there and that he wasn't planning on stepping on anyone's toes. "I was like, Well, I don't want to ask him if I can move," he responded. "That seems silly." Smith said that he didn't have to ask permission, but that it would be wise to just give Reda the heads up. "So I texted him, and I was like, Hey, just wanted to let you know I'm thinking about moving to New York. I hope we can co-exist up there together." Reda called him and told him how much he appreciated the gesture. "He was very, very happy. Because another photographer had moved there and not done that, and they never got along. They still don't. I'm glad I did that." So whenever Mehring found himself near Reda's place (which was often because Reda lived across the street from the photo lab they all used), he would hit him up. "And he would always be home, for some reason. And he would make me an espresso because he was all about some coffee, because he's sober, I guess." Before Reda's espresso, Mehring had never drank coffee in his life. "Now I drink it every fucking day, at least twice."

It took Mehring two years to get the Trans-Siberian trip off the ground. In the end, Vans, Zero, Planet Earth, and iPath all contributed to the $30,000 budget. Along with Mehring came Kenny Reed, Jack Sabback, Keegan Sauder, Van Wastell, Kirill ("a skater and writer from Russia who helped us out immensely"), and Mike Fox, the filmer. They began in Moscow, where they knew they could get some footage before heading out into the untested terrain of Siberia and Mongolia. In a tiny compartment ("About 6'x5'x8', I'd say"), the crew rode 40+ hours on the train, passing "wooden villages in vast forests" and eating "the nastiest Ramen noodles you can imagine." Their first stop was Omsk, where they found a surprising number of skate spots. Next was Novosibirsk, where they were met by Rollerbladers, one of whom said to them, "You are in Siberia. Are you scared?" Mehring wasn't sure what that was supposed to mean, but when they all arrived at the apartment the locals had arranged for them, they found that "someone had spray-painted 'Kill the USA' on the wall next to the front door." They were taken to an "American restaurant," where they witnessed a fight and ate another terrible meal ("I had spaghetti with cinnamon sauce, I think"). "This is what I thought Siberia would be like," Mehring wrote about Novosibirsk. "The place was rugged, full of pollution and sketchy drunks on street corners."

After a minor delay involving Reed's visa, they rode to Ulaanbaatar, the biggest city in Mongolia, a poverty-stricken place filled with dirt roads, shanty houses, and vodka drunks. Both Mehring and Mike Fox, the filmer, had their cameras stolen. But it also provided some of the more memorable moments: "We rode horses, camels, yaks, and Keegan held a falcon," Mehring wrote, "and we also had horsemeat. It was a pretty ridiculous day; we were all just looking at each other riding horses across a river in Mongolia saying, 'This is a skate trip??? Why can't they all be like this?'"

Then they headed for China where the five-week journey ended.

At a Christmas party in 2008, Mehring found himself in conversation with a woman who seemed interested in his travels. When he explained what he did for a living, she told him that she was an editor for *National Geographic*'s book division. "We're always looking for youth content," she told him. "Do you think you'd have enough material for a book?" Perhaps he did, he said. They set up a meeting.

"I had never had a meeting in my life," he told me.

Mehring brought a Kodak paper box full of prints to his meeting with Susan Hitchcock, the woman he'd met at the party. Wearing a hoodie, Mehring was surprised to discover that he would be talking to around ten people from the *NatGeo* staff. While they enjoyed his photos, they wondered what the angle was. Afterward, Hitchcock emailed him and said that it wasn't going to happen right then. "There were some higher-ups," Mehring explains, "they were telling Susan, you know, 'We don't really do skating. That's not our thing.'" But Hitchcock believed in the project and told Mehring that they had to figure out how his images fit into the NatGeo mission. How were his photos—how was skateboarding—benefiting the world in some way?

The meeting had a profound impact on Mehring's perception of his career. "That was when it kind of clicked for me," he said, "because I didn't know what I was doing as far as the direction of my work. But that was when I started thinking about my body of work as a meaningful thing, and not just a guy trying to fill pages every month." Moreover, his ambition expanded with this newfound sense of purpose. He pushed the traveling more with a focused intensity. He went to Madagascar, Morocco, Ethiopia, and Uganda; Kazakhstan, Azerbaijan, Iran, and Afghanistan; India, Vietnam, South Korea, Japan, Taiwan, and Cambodia; Colombia, Brazil, Bolivia, and Argentina. During this time it struck him what his work was all about: "It dawned on me, which was so obvious, I think, had I not been so inside of skating. But I was like, oh, skating is a global language. It's a common culture that we all share. Big picture, right? You can go anywhere with a skateboard and have a friend, literally fucking anywhere, in any country."

He's right: skateboarding is an international passport to a community. When I flew to England for a study abroad program at Oxford, our flight was diverted to Scotland because of some snowy weather. At the airport waiting to learn how we were going to get back to London, our original destination, I hit the bar and had a few drinks. More time must have passed than I realized because suddenly this British dude nudges me and says, "Hey, we've gotta go, mate." A fellow passenger from my flight. I thanked him profusely (and tipsily), because if he hadn't come to get me, I would have totally missed the bus that took us to a hotel for the night. After I expressed my gratitude, he was like, "It's cool, man. I saw your board, so." Then it made sense. He was a skater. Skaters help skaters. If I hadn't been lugging around my board with me, he probably would never have registered my presence and thus wouldn't have made sure I made the bus. But he saw my board, so.

Mehring contacted Hitchcock again (with whom he'd kept in contact in the interim three years) and told her his angle. NatGeo was interested, but they worried about the financial risk. Could Mehring acquire a sponsor for the book? Though Mehring believed that this new hurdle would prevent the book from happening, he stumbled onto a sponsor while he was working in India. Levi's wanted to start advertising in the magazine and happened to have people in Bangalore, where Mehring was staying at the time. Levi's had funded a skatepark there and wanted to see if Mehring could cover the groundbreaking. So Mehring attended the construction, snapped some photos, and ended up having drinks with Levi's marketing director, who told him that Levi's had given a ton of money for their skate program (which included building the skatepark) and that he had a lot left over that he didn't know what to do with. Boom. Mehring got himself a sponsor for his book.

Which is how *Skate the World: Photographing One World of Skateboarding* was born. Featuring 200 images from Mehring and a few other photographers, a foreword by Tony Hawk, and brief features on particularly interesting locations, *Skate the World* is the most comprehensive representation of skateboarding's global force. There are a lot of great collections of skate photos—by greats like Giovanni Reda and Mike Blablac, and magazines like *Thrasher*—but Mehring's communicate the enormity of skating's reach, its diverse influence in every culture on Earth.

It also captures Mehring's sensibility. His photos are just as interested in the world around the trick as they are the trick itself. Many of his images stand far back from the skater, allowing the surrounding terrain to become as pivotal to the photo's success. And he's attracted to candidness, those little moments in skating—kids waiting their turn at a park, a skater pushing on the street, a dude setting up his board—that speak to the intimate mundanity of the lives of most skaters. *Skate the World* is quite an accomplishment, representing as it does thirteen years of Mehring's work. Published in 2015, the book was part of the lengthy, multi-faceted legitimization of skateboarding, which culminated in the 2020 Olympics in Tokyo. National Geographic is a storied institution; their stamp of approval on skateboarding as something that benefits the world is a small but important step. GrindMedia, the company that owned *Skateboarder* and *Transworld*, announced in 2013 that *Skateboarder* would cease its print publication and transition to digital. After only three issues in that format, the magazine shut down permanently.

"What happened was," Mehring told me, "the publisher looked at the numbers and saw that *Transworld* had better ad clients and rates. They decided to can *Skateboarder,* but *Skateboarder* had been making a profit. The most important thing was on the ground level everyone likes *Skateboarder* and nobody likes *Transworld*, but the publisher couldn't see that and so they canned the wrong one, in my opinion."

The primacy of skate magazines has disappeared. When Mehring was coming up, photography was "the Holy Grail:" "You know, I was, of course, obsessed with the videos, but to me, the magazines were where it was at. I mean, you could go out with a pro skater with no filmer and get a photo and that was considered fine." Photos and footage were "equally important." But now, "footage is way more important. A lot of guys go out and never shoot a photo ever. A lot of guys have entire careers without a photo being taken."

Even though Instagram ostensibly began as a photo-sharing app, for skateboarders video reigns supreme, which has functioned as the death knell for skate photography, while also lessening the importance of full-length videos—shit, even video parts. "The song is king on Spotify," Mehring said, "where it used to be the album. It's the same thing. Now the trick is king."

The decline of images in favor of video—as well as the loss of financial stability in the field—makes him "a little sad," but Mehring isn't one to harp on the past. Since leaving *Skateboarder* and publishing *Skate the World*, Mehring has done what many of skateboarding's best photographers have done: turned to commercial work for brands like Adidas and ADT Security. Other so-called action sports like surfing and climbing and cycling are part of his repertoire now. He shot bands for the House of Vans venue in Brooklyn before it closed in 2018. He's also become interested in cinematography. Illegal Civ's recent movie *North Hollywood* made him think he could get an idea of his mounted. In 2020, Mehring also had a son, Oliver, who has become the organizing principle of his life. So even though he's now freelancing after years of retainers, he's more than ever dedicated to financial security.

And he still shoots skate photos, of course. In fact, one of our conversations occurred while he drove to New York for a job. "And then on the way back," he said, "I'm going to stop in DC to shoot a skate photo with Bobby Worrest, who I haven't seen in years. I just came up with an idea for an angle that's never been done at Pulaski." (Pulaski is a plaza in DC that's officially known as Freedom Plaza but is referred to as Pulaski by skaters because of the statue of General Pulaski, an American Revolutionary War hero, that stands in the park.) The concept for the photo, Mehring explains, comes from incorporating inspiration from his other gigs.

"Have you seen the Biggie doc?" he asked me. "A lot of times I think that what it is—it's people who are getting inspiration from other areas of life, like their world is bigger than like, just the thing they're good at. And that's like they talked about that in the Biggie documentary, when he was getting inspiration from the country music scene in Jamaica, which I didn't even know is a thing. But apparently his mom, like grew up in Jamaica and she'd would go there with him every year. And like, there was a scene music scene there that he was part of. Anyway. But that's kind of like where his musical sensibility came from, in a way. And that's why he was different. And that he stood out." He also added that Biggie was just super fucking good at what he did.

"Anyway," he continued, "this photo of Bobby is informed by the fact that I've been shooting surfing a little bit lately. So I'm taking some surfing sensibilities into this photo of Bobby, and that's exciting to me, because I've never done that before. And I don't care where the photo goes. I'm super stoked to just put it on my own Instagram if I can't find a home for it. And you know? That feels great."

3 VIDEO DAYS

A kid who lived down the street from me during my elementary school days loved watching highlight videos of NBA stars. These were fast-edited compilations set to up-tempo jock jams of Michael Jordan, Penny Hardaway, John Stockton, and other players performing their greatest and most cinematic moves. Some sections of these videos focused on a single person, while others were organized around a theme, like, say, dunks or assists or game-winners. We ate these videos up, and then, humming the bombastic music, we'd go out to my friend's driveway and imitate what we saw on his hoop.

It's understandable for a non-skater to compare skate videos to those highlight compilations, as they are what skate videos most superficially resemble: a selection of a skater's most difficult tricks, set to music. Moreover, skate videos have a similar effect: they inspire skaters to go out and skate, often with the soundtrack stuck in our heads. But there are crucial differences that ultimately make a skate video closer to high art than fan edit.

The first difference: Michael Jordan didn't sink that game-winner or dunk that ball for the highlight reel. He did it to win the game. The fact that his greatest plays wind up edited together to inspire young players is secondary. In fact, a basketball player's skills in a practice setting are rarely as celebrated as their actions during competitions. Jordan, for instance, was among the best dunkers in the history of the game, and on an empty court he could perform some remarkably dexterous maneuvers. But his most iconic moments are those that—even though the plays, as an isolated act, aren't as physically impressive as complex dunks—involve the stakes of the postseason. "The Shot,"—Jordan's game-winner during a playoff game against the Cleveland Cavaliers in 1989—is, after all, just a mid-range jumper, something Jordan could probably do with his eyes closed; but in the high-pressure situation of a ticking clock and a win-or-lose outcome, his bucket becomes legendary.

Skaters, on the other hand, film their tricks specifically and exclusively for their video parts, and although competitions certainly exist in skateboarding, such footage is never included. The one caveat is that street skaters don't use clips from skate parks, which are viewed as too perfectly designed for anything performed in them to be taken as gospel. To have truly landed a trick, you've got to take it to the streets. (Park skaters—i.e., those who specialize in riding bowls or vert ramps—are obviously allowed to use park footage, as there are no real-world equivalents to these giant obstacles.) The streets, more so than any contest, are the competitive terrain of skateboarding. Street spots, designed as they are for other purposes, abound in challenges: security, police, pedestrians, limiting architecture, awkward angles, etc. Many skaters even treat tricks landed at parks as something other than official, much the way an NBA player making 15 three-pointers in a scrimmage wouldn't then hold the record for threes in a game.

Another crucial distinction between skate videos and highlight reels: skaters often participate in their creation. Though of course an NBA player can generate their own edits of their greatest on-court accomplishments, it is more likely that a fan would make these. Pro basketball players are more apt to produce something akin to Jordan's ESPN documentary *The Last Dance* than they are a four-minute hype video. But skaters spend years working on these song-length parts. And to varying degrees, they are involved in the final product. They might pick the song, decide the order of tricks, and contribute to the overall tone of the piece. This is why skaters see the video part as the fundamental form in skateboarding. It is the band's album, the comic's special, the writer's novel. A video part represents not only years of filming extremely difficult tricks, but also hours of thought and experimentation on the *presentation* of those tricks. It is, as Rob Gordon (John Cusack's character in *High Fidelity*) says of making a mixtape, a "delicate art." And throughout the history of skateboarding, some skaters have elevated the form to new levels, deepening its potential meaning and expanding its possibilities in ways no one could have foreseen. This is the story of one such skater, and one such video part.

*   *   *

Somewhere in between Mark Suciu's first major introduction to the skate world—in 2010's Habitat video "Origin"—and now, he has managed to put out numerous video parts, film endless clips for Instagram and cameo appearances, compete in dozens of contests around the globe, and travel with various teams to every continent on the planet. This productivity is made all the more impressive when you add in another significant achievement made during that same period: earning a bachelor's degree in English from Temple University.

In 2011 Suciu released "Cross Continental," one of the earlier and more influential stand-alone video parts. Before the internet dominated everything, video parts were, as the phrase suggests, parts of longer videos, usually organized around a company or a crew or a skate shop that put the project together. By 2010, skaters like Paul Rodriguez and Shane O'Neill came out with solo video parts, rendering the name a misnomer and the skate world forever altered. Now, though full-lengths still exist, most pros and ams release their parts individually, through outlets like *Thrasher* or The Berrics or Jenkem or the YouTube channel of whatever sponsor is behind them. Suciu's "Cross Continental" solidified his stardom, but at only twenty years old, he was ambivalent about his future as a skateboarder.

It started with a line from "Cross Continental." A line is a sequence of tricks done in a row in the same clip, and it's a hallmark of not only skate videos but contests as well. Being able to demonstrate consistency with tricks—i.e., showing that you can do multiple ones in a row without fucking up— is just as important as the degree of difficulty of those tricks. One of the most iconic lines was done by Mike Carroll, one of the greatest street skaters ever. It comes at the beginning of his part from *Transworld*'s video *Modus Operandi* (2000), and it takes place at the San Francisco Public Library. It's a five-trick line, and for Suciu, it "stood out to me as like the best line that had ever been filmed and the most put together. And I wanted to replicate that in some way."

He said this to me over Zoom, about a half an hour into what would turn out to be a three-and a-half-hour-long conversation. Suciu, besides being one of the world's best skateboarders, is also of a literary bent: he's well spoken, well read, and invested in his continual education. All of which is to say that we got along splendidly. At one point, for instance, he paused for a moment and said, "I gotta take a screenshot because we have the same editions of Proust in our background." And sure enough, we both own Penguin's new translations of *In Search of Lost Time*, a seven-volume novel by the French writer Marcel Proust. It's a notoriously lengthy (some 4,200 pages and 1,200,000 words in total) and thorny text—Proust is famous for his long, periodic sentences and his remarkably assiduous examinations of society, art, and love. Not exactly something you'd find on the average person's bookshelf, but it's definitely something you'd discover in the home of anyone with an interest in literature, especially fiction. And Suciu, going one step further, learned French and has read Proust in his original language.

So when Suciu wanted to replicate Mike Carroll's line from *Modus Operandi*, he did so in a decidedly esoteric way—the way a writer might make complex allusions to other texts. Because Suciu didn't just go to the SF Public Library and film a line (which alone would have constituted an adequate shout-out), he referenced other skaters in it too, so that each trick was an allusion to a single skater and the line as a whole an allusion to Carroll. Although conceiving and filming the line satisfied a particularly meta-textual aspect of Suciu's brain, there was one major problem: "I realized, like, wait a second: nobody's going to *get* this." His deeply considered references were too arcane, impossible for a viewer to spot, in part because there wasn't anything signaling their existence. How would someone catch such deep cuts without being made aware that they should be looking for them? What this indicated to Suciu, though, was that maybe he was aiming his intellectual propensities in the wrong direction. Maybe he was applying his tools to the wrong machine.

Plus, he was young, on his own for the first time, and feeling the effects of his sudden stardom. "I'm alone a lot," he said of the period. "I'm staying up late for the first time in my life. Like staying up all through the night and just like reading and reading. And then I get hurt and couldn't skate. So it's like a lot of alone time and seeing places empty for the first time in my life and feeling a deep, a deep, a deep—I don't know—sense of . . . I wouldn't go so far as to say a sense of loss, but just like, there's a lot of things that are lacking and it's really affecting me."

Suciu's example of "seeing places empty for the first time" struck me as such an apt encapsulation of the ennui of maturation. A young person coming of age in the real world *does* see an alternate version than the one they were first introduced to. Staying out late in my early 20s, I recognized the incongruity of barren cityscapes —it wasn't that I found anything particularly profound about the image of an empty street; rather, it was an awareness of my recently obtained opportunity to see it. Living on my own, being an adult, I now had access to new angles of the environment around me, more telling angles, ones that added up to more nuanced portraits, which meant that everything I thought I knew was being (and would continue to be) redefined, amended, or completely contradicted. And there was an air of melancholy attached to those realizations, one I can't fully explain but which is succinctly captured by Suciu's phrase, "seeing places empty for the first time."

For Suciu, these kinds of growing pains lead to serious self-reflection:

Then I was asking deeper questions, like, maybe I should help the world. Maybe I need to abolish homelessness— just like these huge questions, you know, because it seemed like I had my whole life in front of me and every possibility was out there. And then it just made things take longer for me to decide on like, Oh, wait, *this* is not my life. *This* is my life.

Such contemplation at that age, in the face of a burgeoning skateboarding career, struck me as significant, courageous even, but when I suggested as much, Suciu was pretty quick to dismiss that interpretation. "It sounds funny to me, for you to say that it was courageous, because looking back on that time, I was probably the biggest shithead kid, you know? Like, so unapproachable, so unfriendly; just completely living out an idealized version of themselves." It wasn't merely his self-regard; it was his seriousness. "I had no sense of humor, is the thing," he explained. "And I was very privileged. I was very privileged, and it was the privilege that allowed the confidence to downplay the success, I think, or to just neutralize it and to be like, okay, I'm here. What next? You know?"

At the time, though, his sense of personal direction still felt undetermined, despite his propulsive success as a skateboarder, so in 2014, Suciu enrolled at Temple University, majoring in English. "I went into undergrad thinking I wanted to study poetry," he said. "I wanted to be an artist. And I thought poetry was the greatest art or something." But he quickly realized that although he admired poetry, fiction was the form that most spoke to him. "[Poetry] was kind of a recent thing. Whereas I'd spent my whole life writing novels and thinking of stories and even the poems that I liked the most were narrative. And that was a lot of the poetry that I was writing. So then to move into fiction, it was just like, 'Oh yeah, I'm definitely better at this.' And then I never really looked back."

Besides the conflict of "Should I be a pro skater or pursue writing?" what he was really dealing with was the youthful fallacy of impatience, of thinking everything must be figured out immediately. "It was fueled by this inner desire that I just wanted to like break away and do new things and like not go with the flow whatsoever so that I could become this vision of myself." He goes on:

> But then once I graduated and realized that there were going to be things that I couldn't just will into existence. I had to go with the flow in order to actually live my life. Then I kind of reached a point where I'm at now, where it's like, I do want to write, but I have no idea what's going to happen in my life. All I know is that I have to skate and I have to continue doing the best that I can just so that I lay the foundations for a fulfilling next ten years, you know, once this is done. And hopefully it means writing, hopefully it means fiction. If not, you know, maybe it means some other sort of writing or maybe it means going back to school, but whatever it is, I'm just waiting for the time when I can listen to myself and be like, okay, yeah, that's who I am.

Suciu then experienced a crisis of identity during which skateboarding didn't feel like it was offering him the kind of expression he yearned to pursue. In college, he developed his fascination with literature into an interest in writing fiction, but also settled the skating-versus-writing battle by not declaring a winner but rather learning that the two are not mutually exclusive. He can skate; he can write. Life is big enough for both.

What's particularly interesting here is what came of these epiphanies: Suciu's 11-minute video part from 2019 "Verso," which for my money is the most complex, the most unique, the most accomplished video part ever made. And a big part of its success lies in those seemingly polar components of Suciu's self: art and action. In "Verso," Suciu combines them, extracts the most interesting and useful elements of each and creates something remarkable as a result.

So, remember that line from "Cross Continental" that Suciu realized was too obscure for anyone to understand? Well, after years of growth and time spent studying the mechanics of literature, Suciu found a way to do something even more esoteric, even more structurally experimental—but this time he figured out a way to signal it to the viewer. He wasn't hiding art in his skateboarding anymore. His skateboarding *became* his art.

To begin with: no video part is worth a damn if the tricks aren't great. This could mean that they're new, heretofore unseen tricks, or that they're exceptionally performed ones (or, ideally, both). We have to *want* to watch the skating; good editing or a well-chosen song only take you so far. By this metric, Suciu's "Verso" is one of the most dynamic edits any skater has ever put out. The dude just has a different level of skill, a one-of-a-kind approach to spots, and an imagination for variations that confound the mind.

This is as good a time as any to explain a little bit about Suciu's skate style, and specifically to elucidate what he refers to as "pretzel tricks." A pretzel trick involves motions and spins that push the body around awkwardly. Typically, they're tricks where a skater 180s in one direction and reverts back the opposite way, sort of undoing the first turn. Or, a skater may merely 180 out of a grind or manual in the most challenging direction. You must possess excess amounts of dexterity and board control in order to do these tricks, and because they're so difficult, many skaters can't make them look good, and as a consequence they're uncommon. Pro skaters like Karl Watson and Tim O'Connor did pretzel tricks, and Suciu noticed. "I realized that pretzel tricks were very under done," he said, "and there was a lot left to do." It's also an aesthetic thing: "It's just because I think it looks so good."

Suciu has made an art out of pretzel tricks. He has taken ugly and strained-looking tricks and turned them into an effortless style. It's akin to transforming a handful of rusty instruments into a symphony of beautiful music. Or maybe the more accurate metaphor would be some stunning piece of machinery—how inert, technical components can combine to become a gorgeous invention. Suciu's skating often involves back-breaking, body-contorting tricks, but his style is characterized by its apparent effortlessness; it's an astonishing pair of facts. Suciu is so known for such tricks that there is a pretzel trick that bears his name: the Suciu grind—a bs 180 to switch fs salad grind switch bs 180 out—which requires acrobatic contortion just to describe, let alone perform.

The fundamental skill required to do a pretzel trick is fast footwork. Dexterity matters, of course, but quick feet make it possible. Suciu's skating is a masterclass in speedy feet. On The Berrics, there is a series called "Ninja Training," in which skaters attempt to do a trick up onto a long, concrete ledge, do another trick while riding on top, and then do another trick off. The idea is that such exercises help with foot control, by making the skater do something they ordinarily wouldn't. Well, Suciu does this kind of thing all the time, on all sorts of obstacles. It is not training for him; it's his style.

Suciu's mastery of pretzels complements his rarefied approach to spots. He just sees skate terrain differently. The nuance required to articulate just how his perception differs from other skaters is perhaps beyond my capabilities (without reverting to some hopelessly technical jargon), but here's one way to express it: when the podcast *The Nine Club*—a show featuring pro skaters and industry people—reviewed Suciu's "Verso" part, they repeatedly said things like, "Any normal person would [look at that spot] and go, 'Ah, shit.' But he's like, 'No, I got a trick for it,'" or "How do you see that spot and go, 'Yeah, *that's* what I want to do?'" They compare Suciu to Marc Johnson, one of the most technically gifted, innovatively oriented, and uniquely visionary skaters of all time. Justin Eldridge (who rode for Chocolate, the sister company to Girl, who Johnson skated for) said of the comparison, "Having skated with Marc Johnson all these years—like going on tours with him. It feels like that. He would just go to spots, and you would never think of [doing this trick]—but he did." A few minutes later, Eldridge asked, "Do you think that [Suciu] knows . . . that he's just like the best? Do you think he knows, like, I literally think about skateboarding differently than anyone around me?"

These last five paragraphs have all been precursors to this: in terms of tricks alone—degree of difficulty, variation, and style—"Verso" ranks as an all-time video part. By my count—which is an especially difficult task, as Suciu does a number of combos: if he does a three-trick combo (like, say, ollieing over a chain onto a sculpture, doing a hardflip on the sculpture, and then big-spinning back over the chain to get off), does that count as one trick or three?—there are over 140 tricks in an 11-minute and-36-second video. Here are some of the figures from *Thrasher Magazine*'s breakdown of the part into numbers: Suciu flips into tricks 15 times, and flips out seven times; he spins his body a grand total of 18,720 degrees; he does 22 pretzel tricks (or, as *Thrasher* refers to them, "tricks with a back-breaking awkward rotation"); and in his lines, Suciu performs 23.814 tricks per minute. A video part with this many tricks is extremely rare. Consider, for instance, something that Kyle Beachy pointed out in a widely read essay on "Verso": Nyjah Huston's "Til Death" part was also 11 minutes but contained only half the tricks (71). Suciu could have easily split "Verso" into two or even three different parts and released them months or even years apart. He could have rested on these achievements, taken a break, made more money, and no one would have been the wiser.

But true art isn't practical. It isn't interested in spreading itself out for the sake of economy, or relaxation, or careerism. Great art maximizes its power in any way it can. It wants everything you've got, and more. A measure of an artist can be found in the unnecessary work, in the fudgeable details, in the spots the common eye overlooks. Suciu stuffed "Verso" full of tricks, but its brilliance extends beyond its volume and the difficulty of the tricks.

Concept videos aren't new. In fact, skateboarding has a healthy history of high-concept productions. In the 1980s, the Bones Brigade made what were pretty much feature films. *The Search for Animal Chin*, for instance, has a plot, production value, a script, acting—the whole nine. Sure, the story is flimsy and simplistic (and, as we've discussed, a little racist), but it's still a narrative. *The End*, a 1998 video from Birdhouse, forgoes any plot for the whole video and instead gives each skater a concept of his own. Steve Berra's part is done as if he's being chased by some monster; Tony Hawk appears as a matador; Jeremy Klein and Heath Kirchart wear suits and use a ramp to skate business signs and bus stops and a shed that's on fire (not really sure what the concept behind this part is, to be honest—but it's one of my favorite video parts nonetheless).

There are videos organized around particular terrain. "Flatbar Frenzy" is comprised of Torey Pudwill skating various kinds of rails. Almost's *Cheese and Crackers* takes place entirely in an abandoned warehouse, in which Daewon Song and Chris Haslam skate a single mini-ramp. There are, too, parts with subtler ideas behind them: Jerry Hsu in *Stay Gold* (Emerica 2010), for instance, does only switch tricks.

"Verso," though, experiments with something in a way no other video ever has before: its structure. It's made up of four parts, each with its own song. The first and fourth song are by Beirut, while the two middle songs are both by French bands. The final section's assembly is innovative to such a degree that it's actually hard to explain. Maybe starting with Suciu's own thought process will help here. "So that summer before school started," Suciu told me, "I was in Japan with no service, only apps. And I had the Poetry Foundation app going, reading a lot of haikus because I was in Japan, but also just a lot of poetry, like when we were waiting for the train and stuff like that. And then I was writing some haikus for my friend to send back as a letter, but then also trying to write—it was like a five-by-five poem, like five word or syllable line and five lines of them. The rhyme was going to descend through. It looked exactly like the way 'Verso' looks on the page where it kind of crosses through."

What Suciu's describing here is a literary term called "chiasmus," a rhetorical device in which the ideas, grammar, and sometimes the words in the beginning of a phrase are reversed in the ending of the phrase. Technically, "antimetabole" is the term for a phrase in which the same words recur, as in "Fair is foul, and foul is fair" from Shakespeare's *Macbeth* and "Beauty is truth, truth beauty" from John Keats's "Ode to a Grecian Urn." Ward Farnsworth, in his authoritative *Farnsworth's Classical English Rhetoric* (from which all of my examples come), has this to say about such hair splitting:

> Some commentators call reversal of the same words *antimetabole* and reserve the term *chiasmus* for the reversals that are purely structural. In keeping with this book's preference for simple terminology and distaste for distinctions that aren't worth the bother for the typical user, we will call all these reversals by the same name— *chiasmus*; but the reader with a taste for jargon, a need for precision, or a fear of pedants is duly notified that more words are available.

A "purely structural" chiasmus looks something like this line from *Measure for Measure*: "Some rise by sin, and some by virtue fall." Or this line from *Othello*: "But O, what damned minutes tells he o'er / Who dotes, yet doubts; suspects, yet strongly loves!"

It may seem silly that I'm explicating this term so assiduously, but there is a reason: the final section of Suciu's "Verso" is structured like a series of chiasmus's and antimetaboles all nestled inside of each other. It consists of seven clips of two-trick lines, for a total of fourteen tricks.

The first trick is simple: a frontside 50-50 on a ledge. The fourteenth and final trick is also a frontside 50-50. So these are duplicates of each other. The second trick is a nollie frontside 180 heelflip to fakie 5-0, revert (this last term, in this instance, is technically a fakie backside 180, which is usually referred to as a half-cab, but here it's actually a revert, which just means returning to the stance you began in). The thirteenth trick is a nollie backside 180 heelflip to fakie nosegrind to backside 180 out. These two tricks— unlike the two 50-50s—are opposites: he turns opposite directions and grinds on opposite trucks. Moving inward from both directions (the beginning and the end), the tricks reflect and refract each other deliberately. As in, Suciu chose the tricks *because* they mirrored each other, because, to his literary mind, they *rhymed*. But he didn't know all of this from the onset. When he initially began filming, the tricks came as they often do, as a natural progression of his skills and interests. "It's purely practical," he said. "The fact that it all came to some higher meaning in 'Verso' definitely surprised me, but I was trying." Rumblings of such an ambitious idea began when he landed the thirteenth trick described above. But he landed it as a skatepark, which, as discussed, doesn't really count. "Then I was in Buenos Aires skating with the Adidas team. And I did the nollie halfcab heel, fakie 5-0 revert, the trick that Günes Özdogan does in his Habitat part . . . But I did it at a skatepark." Because he'd done both tricks at parks but wanted them in his part, on the flight home from Argentina, he made a list of tricks to figure out where best to do them. "And then it kind of all started."

Seeing them written down in front of him made evident their composition. He thought, "It would be sick if I could somehow put this together into a little section . . . a little movement." Like many constant travelers, Suciu uses the inertia forced upon him during flights to be productive—to write, imagine tricks, plan out missions. During the aloft hours on the return from Argentina, he started planning out the juxtaposed tricks; flying back from Japan, he happened upon a structure. "Verso" was born in the air.

So what? What's the big deal if the tricks in "Verso" reflect each other in chiasmic structure? To begin with, consider Suciu's part as a literary critic would consider it. One question a critic might ask is: How does the structure of this work relate to its content? Take, for instance, a novel with a comparable construction. David Mitchell's *Cloud Atlas* features six narratives nestled inside of each other. It can be visualized like this:

1A—2A—3A—4A—5A—6—5B—4B—3B—2B—1B

Narrative 1 is interrupted halfway through by Narrative 2, which is then interrupted halfway through by 3, and so on until Narrative 6, which stands at the center complete. Then, the novel moves its way back through the stories in reverse order, finishing them. Narrative 1 takes place in the late 19th century, 2 in the 1930s, 3 in the 60s, 4 in the present day, 5 in a distant future, and 6 even beyond that— which is to say that the structural order isn't arbitrary; it's chronological. The theme of *Cloud Atlas* is the vast and intricate interconnectedness of humanity, regardless of era or identity. Mitchell's design, then, reinforces this notion by entwining them. Structure can be just as important as—can indeed be inextricable from— content.

Suciu's fourth movement, recall, features his trademark pretzel tricks, which often require the body to twist one direction only to revert back to the original position. Suciu's body spins 180 degrees one way into a grind and then turns 180 degrees the opposite way. The fundamental nature of these tricks is reinforced by the structure in which they are presented. The mirrored tricks, too, are each reversals of the tricks they reflect. Taken together, the two pretzel tricks combine to form an even bigger pretzel—or, even more aptly, each trick undoes the movements of its mirror.

This is new, deeper territory to which the video part, as a form, has never ventured. Perhaps some skaters will find such advancements minor, or even meaningless, as for them the point of a video part is to showcase a skater's talents and generate stoke—artfulness is secondary at most, a distraction at worst. To these objections one could easily say something about how there's room for many different kinds of video parts; requiring uniformity goes precisely against the skateboarding ethic. But I think there's a more interesting objection: namely, that the more skaters experiment with the form, and the more, like Suciu, they pursue specific tricks toward that end, the faster and more complexly skateboarding will progress. Each video part is a gauntlet, thrown down as both a declaration and a challenge. It declares: *This* is what I can do. It challenges: What can *you* do? And the more freedom skaters have, the more varied and creative the responses will be. Skateboarding thrives on progression; it requires constant development. And skaters like Suciu, and video parts like "Verso," push it grandly forward, so that someone else can come along to pick up the gauntlet, equipped now with the knowledge of what has already been done, which creates an edge around what hasn't and makes the unknown a little easier to visualize and, eventually, land.

4 SHACKLE ME NOT

Victoria Taylor won't go to a skatepark by herself.

Think about that. Taylor is a skateboarding and fashion influencer with nearly 340,000 followers on Instagram. She earns her living traveling, modeling, and skating. She posts videos constantly of her skating with her friends and progressing her skills.

"I was never comfortable going by myself," she told me, "knowing that I was a girl, young, didn't really know how to skate or make my way around a skatepark enough."

When she first moved from Utah to Los Angeles to attend the Fashion Institute of Design & Merchandising, she was eighteen and alone. Skateboarding was her only outlet, and anyone who has ever relocated can attest to how meaningful the activities you love become in those first months of adjustment. And for men, skateboarding functions like a passport to any local community. You go to a skatepark and you've automatically got a handful of friends. Not so for Taylor, or for women in skateboarding generally. When she hit up a park, she was met with suspicion, condescension, and downright antipathy.

"I'm just doing this because I was so depressed in Utah," she said, "and I have nothing but skateboarding here in California. And now you're making me feel bad about it. And I don't even know you. And you're telling me I can't do something. And there's multiple of you. There's not even one of you. So now I feel like I'm not allowed to do this. I started to feel like I couldn't do it because I didn't look a certain way or, you know, I'm a poser." When Jake, her boyfriend at the time, who still lived in Utah, would visit, his presence made things easier for her. "I'd only go to skate parks with him, because I felt accepted if I was with a guy who skated good."

"The one time I went [to skatepark by myself]," she said, was at El Sereno skatepark, which is encased by fences and adjacent to basketball and tennis courts. "I was in the tennis court by myself just sitting down, and my back was facing the walkway. There was a group of five boys walking in going to the skatepark, and I didn't think anything of it. I turned back around and was checking my phone and all the sudden I just get pelted in the back with a water bottle and it exploded all over me. I look back and they were all just running away."

The LA parks were so volatile for her that she drove an hour outside of the city to go to parks that were all but empty. But since there was no guarantee that those parks wouldn't also contain any number of lurking and juvenile but still scary douchebags, Taylor preferred to skate in an alleyway near her apartment. The sad irony of this is impossible to ignore: for her, an alleyway—the cliché location for criminal activity—was preferable to the public park. Such is the lot of women in a patriarchal culture.

But maybe you're thinking, *Big deal! Those were just some stupid kids. Not* all *men would treat her that way.* Here's why that doesn't fucking matter: Taylor's fears stem from a pattern of behavior from men—from catcalling to creepy messages to assaults—and she cannot distinguish between a safe man and an unsafe one, because they all look alike. Men who argue with women about this are not only being total assholes, but they're also confronting the exact wrong person. It is the *men* who do these things, the ones whose terrifying actions lump the "not all men" gang into the "potential murderer" pile, who should be targeted and punished. All Taylor can do is make choices based on her experience.

Moreover, an incident like the water bottle is scary and awful enough, but that is not even the most extreme example, not by a longshot. For over a year, Taylor had a stalker. "I have a big stack of documents of it. He had photos of my face printed out, and he would like ejaculate onto photos of me and send me photos of that. And then he knew where I lived downtown." Every day, this man posted "paragraphs and paragraphs" of comments on her photos with the possessive, entitled mix of amity and antipathy typical of stalkers. This illustrates just how wide the gap is between the experience of those who identify as female and those who identify as male, just as much as it shows the gap between celebrities and non-celebrities. The idea of a stranger commenting on my photos every single day with threatening and accusatory messages, with creepily knowledgeable insinuations, is totally foreign to me, as I'm sure it is for most cisgender men. Taylor, of course, has a considerable following, but 1) that doesn't make the idea of a stalker any less terrifying, just as 2), it doesn't make Taylor any more deserving of having one, and 3) Taylor's experience here is tragically common.

And again, the situation got worse:

[The stalker] saw me at the Venice curbs one time when I was with some friends, and I just recognized his voice. And it felt like—and I hope I don't sound evil; I have a therapist and the way that she explained this to me was I felt, like I had gotten raped, but I didn't physically get raped. It felt like I had something completely stolen or violated from me. And it's like something that I felt like maybe I was overreacting about, but it's something that no one would understand unless they were put in that same position. And unfortunately, guys will never understand that and to some guys that can come off as I'm being extra or I'm just doing this for attention.

Before moving on with the story, I just want to note something about the above quote. Consider how much equivocating Taylor does here, how almost apologetic she is about explaining her experience. She has been conditioned to expect push back from men who simply don't believe what she says about how something felt or what it did to her. It is infuriating to imagine men out there hearing this story and dismissing it as "extra" or "for attention." It is absolutely wild that some people think they can actually be an authority on someone else's life. Taylor felt physically violated by the appearance of a stalker who jerked off onto photos of her and then sent those images to her. His every interaction with her was steeped in sexual violence and possession. So the mere image of this man in the flesh, standing in front of her, would *of course* conjure up a sense of sexual violation, of intrusion, which is what rape is. Taylor is *not* overreacting here.

I say this not to admonish her for believing she needs to justify her choice of words but to highlight the effect that men's constant dismissal of women's experiences has on women. It makes them question the legitimacy of their reactions, which oftentimes means they won't seek the treatment they need or they won't go to the police (who probably wouldn't believe them anyway)—all of which perpetuates the problems. Men, by not believing women, are actively ensuring that sexual violence, in all its forms, will continue unabated.

Back to the Venice curbs: "Luckily," she told me, she was with her friend Le'andre Sanders (often referred to, like Taylor, by his Instagram handle @skategoat). "He didn't even know I had this stalker at the time, but he saw the look on my face when I heard that guy's voice, and he just knew and chased the guy off." A few hours later, at the Venice skatepark, "I look over and the guy's standing right there, and he's just smiling at me. And I just screamed and left my board and ran across the skatepark. He followed me, and he was like, You don't want to come surfing? Like, not even making any type of sense. Then Le'andre just stood up in the middle of the Venice park and was like, This guy's a fucking pedophile! Luckily, it's Le'andre's skatepark and all the locals know him, so they all chased him out."

So she won't go to skateparks alone, but she will—and often does—go with a crew of other girl skaters. (Note: Taylor uses the term "girl skater" and generally refers to women as "girls," so in keeping with her verbiage, I am also using this language.) Feeling frustrated by the skatepark scene, she went through all the people that the Instagram account Girls Shred followed. "Then I would literally click on girl's accounts and see if they live in California and I remember one day, Hillary Shanks was reposting and I was like, 'Who is that? That's Stoner Skatepark.'" Taylor DM'd Shanks, followed her, and eventually went skating with her. Jennifer Charlene joined the crew too, and soon the three were "inseparable." "We were going to every skate park," she said, "because we were the three girls and we had each other. We would even just go on the corner and skate flat or something. That started to help build my mentality of: Okay, there's other girls skaters like me."

Armed with a crew, Taylor skated more regularly and developed quicker. Any skater will tell you how vast the difference is between skating alone and skating with friends. Friends motivate you, compel you onward, even challenge you. Skating alone is practice; skating with friends is skating. This development she tracked via her Instagram page, which began to grow considerably. One of the most refreshing aspects of Taylor's videos is how willing she is to post clips of herself eating shit. Taylor is—and we'll move into this in a bit—a very fashionable person. She dresses impeccably, with a confident and vibrant style. Her aesthetic has a lot in common with skate style—loose fits, skateable gear, beanies, etc.—and thus has some conventionally male influences, but it is undeniably feminine. She wears makeup, styles her hair exquisitely, and often her shirts expose her midriff. She has, in effect, combined skate fashion with high fashion. Most people whose clothes are as fresh as hers—and for whom fashion matters so much—wouldn't want to fuck up their gear by falling roughly onto concrete. But Taylor posts these kinds of videos all the time. Like, after her fashion sense, it's the thing I most associate with her. And I fucking love it. I love how she simultaneously upends the stereotype of highly fashionable femininity—the kind that wouldn't want to tear and stain and destroy their clothes—and challenges the conventional look of a skateboarder. Her aesthetic says to whomever watches her skate: You don't have to conform to the classic skater look to be a skater; and you can engage in dirty and dangerous and male-dominated activities without sacrificing an ounce of your style or femininity. Taylor is a positive influence in skateboarding.

There's this classical pianist named Yuja Wang, who is known not only for her virtuoso skills but also for the dramatic and stylish attire she wears during her concerts. Here's how Janet Malcolm opens her 2016 profile of Wang in *The New Yorker*:

What is one to think of the clothes the twenty-nine-year-old pianist Yuja Wang wears when she performs—extremely short and tight dresses that ride up as she plays, so that she has to tug at them when she has a free hand, or clinging backless gowns that give the impression of near-nakedness (accompanied in all cases by four-inch-high stiletto heels)? In 2011, Mark Swed, the music critic of the *L.A. Times*, referring to the short and tight orange dress Yuja wore when she played Rachmaninoff's Third Piano Concerto at the Hollywood Bowl, wrote that "had there been any less of it, the Bowl might have been forced to restrict admission to any music lover under 18 not accompanied by an adult." Two years later, the *New Criterion* critic Jay Nordlinger characterized the "shorter-than short red dress, barely covering her rear," that Yuja wore for a Carnegie Hall recital as "stripper-wear." Never has the relationship between what we see at a concert and what we hear come under such perplexing scrutiny. Is the seeing part a distraction (Glenn Gould thought it was) or is it—can it be—a heightening of the musical experience?

I think Wang is an interesting comparison to Taylor, as they both challenge traditional ideas about gender in their respective fields, both with a highly—even confrontationally—feminine flourish. Taylor doesn't sport high heels or wear tight-fitting dresses when she skates, but Taylor upends the conventions in a similarly stylish manner. And the question about "the seeing part" is also fascinating to me: how much does the style of the skater affect our view of their skateboarding? Is watching someone with dope style but less developed skills more compelling than someone with zero style but lots of talent? There are many more reasons to watch a skater than their tricks. Skaters talk a lot about style in terms of skating—how someone pushes, rolls, pops, lands—but often those with sartorial flare are often derided *because* of their styles. Skaters like Richie Jackson or Stephen Lawyer—who both dress in unique and conspicuous manners—are often dragged for their looks. Hell, people used to talk shit about Dylan Rieder (who died in 2016) because he looked so *good*—like a model, in fact, because, well, he was one.

"I'm wearing what's in my closet," Taylor told me. Her clothes, in other words, are not some direct attempt to distinguish herself, or to create a career, which strikes me as true not only because Taylor said it and I have no reason not to believe her, but also because of this: How is it possible for a person to set out to gain notoriety from *only* their style—particularly in an environment that isn't wholly revolved *around* style—and then actually succeed in doing that? How likely is it that Taylor's explosion on Instagram was planned out? How could anyone have that kind of foresight? "Those are people who are just mad; they're mad, and they haven't seen it before. So it's new to them, and that makes them uncomfortable."

Her role as an online personality began with her high school boyfriend Jacob, who introduced her to skating. He noticed the positive reception of her social media posts. His initial idea, though, was a YouTube channel about a skateboarding couple. Taylor had reservations. Her home life wasn't a nurturing environment, and she didn't have a lot of friends at the time. "I'm not trying to put my only good relationship that I have, throw it out there and invite everybody in it." But Jacob, according to Taylor, had different motivations: "He just wanted to be famous." The dynamic "started to build into this like toxic thing, and I started to feel like, 'Man, maybe you don't like me. Maybe you kind of just want to use me to like, get a free ride off me. And that scares me.'"

Although they continued to date after Taylor moved to LA, their relationship soured as Taylor's following grew. By the time she connected with Shanks and Charlene, Taylor's posts were getting shared and seen widely. "Pro skaters were following me," she said. "But the fact that my ex was living in Utah, he felt like he was maybe missing out on opportunities for me. And he started to feel like I was taking his opportunities."

One of those pro skaters was Steve Berra. A former pro for Birdhouse, Berra has remained a major part of skateboarding via his website The Berrics, which he co-founded with Eric Koston, who is one of the few skaters whose name is familiar to non-skaters. The Berrics is essentially just a private indoor skatepark in LA, in which they film all kinds of content, from weekly series to contests to brief little edits of a single skater ripping the park called Bangin'. The site gained popularity with the creation of Battle at the Berrics (BATB), a game of SKATE tournament (the one that borrowed its rules from Mark Waters, which are pretty much identical, with one significant exception: Last letter gets two tries. Waters's éS Game of Skate always had so many participants that anything that would have extended individual games [like a rule that not only gives a skater another attempt but also often leads to that skater staying in the game and thus extending the contest] couldn't be accommodated. Still, Waters always felt a bit hurt that Berra never acknowledged him as an inspiration for the format of BATB).

Recently, The Berrics has gone from a skatepark that produces in-house content to a marketing arm for companies like Cariuma, a shoe brand, and Sway, an energy drink. Their videos now are so nakedly promotional for an aesthetic I don't care for and companies I'm not interested in that I watch them far less than I used to. Moreover, Berra himself has become embroiled in a few online beefs and controversies, with, for example, a YouTuber who goes by the name Gifted Hater (who, along with Rad Rat, produces some of the most interesting skate content). Berra seems to be losing touch with the younger generations, an inevitable, if unfortunate, development.

Anyway, Berra reached out to Taylor on Instagram and invited her to come to The Berrics. "I remember he was, like, so driven to meet me," she said. "I thought to myself, *What the hell does Steve Berra want to do with me? I can't even kickflip.*"

The assumption many people might make here as to why Berra was so eager to meet Taylor is the same one many (particularly men) made when footage of Taylor skating The Berrics: that he wanted to sleep with her, and that Taylor, from her end, wanted to use Berra to help her career. You can still see similar sentiments expressed on Instagram, on pretty much any clip of Taylor posted by a male or featuring a male. This isn't something that only exists in skateboarding, of course. We constantly accuse ambitious women of "sleeping their way to the top," or some other such phrase. We seem to find it difficult to believe that a woman can succeed on her own merits or that a man can have a genuine interest in a woman that isn't sexual in nature.

"Steve became a father figure to me," Taylor said. "Because everything at home was so crazy. And he saw me as living on my own at such a young age, and not knowing anything, and just being so new to skateboarding and everything. He saw me as just someone that could just get so hurt and like lose it all, because I was someone, at the time, that didn't know how to say no to things and just kind of just took everything that was given to me. And he knew that from me from the start, which is something that's really cool. I see a lot of similarities with my dad and Steve."

It turned out that Berra was more interested in Taylor's fashion sense than her skateboarding. "He wanted me to help him design clothes and stuff for SOVRN [an LA-based skate company]." Berra could plainly see how fashionable Taylor was and, moreover, could probably imagine that she would soon be an influential person with a significant following. Taylor has that written all over her.

"But then people started noticing that I was hanging out with Steve," she said. "It was never, 'Hey, Victoria's this model-looking girl, you guys should follow her.' But that's how people started taking it. They were like, *Why is she—who can't even do a kickflip—always at The Berrics? Are you sleeping with Steve Berra? You're sleeping with Koston?* And it's like, why do I have to be sleeping with a grown man to be able to have my work—that I'm studying in college—recognized? Why? I don't understand the correlation between that."

Women have always been involved in skateboarding. Recall the fact that first issue of *Life*—the one that referred to skateboarding as a "menace"—featured a woman skater on its cover. Her name is Patti McGee, and she was the first female professional skateboarder—a national champion, no less, in 1964. During skateboarding's first fad stage, McGee helped popularize it by appearing on *The Johnny Carson Show* and *What's My Line?* She's a pioneer for skateboarding (recognized, in 2010, by being inducted into the Skateboarding Hall of Fame), even if she's not a household name.

Despite this, women and female-identifying people still face constant antagonism online, at the park, and in the streets. Male skateboarders need to do much, much better.

As Taylor's Instagram led her to friendships and business relationships with people in the skate industry, it also brought her to the attention of people in the fashion world. "A brand from Germany reached out to me," she said, "and they were like, we love your content. We'd love to send you a handmade leather bag." The bag arrived, she took some photos with it, and posted them. "And then I was like, that would be sick if I could just do things like this forever." Soon brands like Dickies and Skullcandy weren't just sending her gear; they were paying her to post. Not huge money at first—a few hundred bucks—but "for a one-hour shoot? I can do that."

Then she got the opportunity to design a run of clothing and griptape for Grizzly, a company started by pro skater Torey Pudwill. Grizzly provides an illustrative example of a skater-run brand. "It started with wax," Pudwill told an interviewer. "We called it Grizzly from the shape of the mold, which was a bear." He got this mold from a friend's mom, who used it for baking. As a kid hanging around Skatelab, a well-known indoor park in Simi Valley, Pudwill started selling griptape he'd been hooked up with by Arcade Skateboards. It was a hustle, not a business, and when he got sponsored and pursued his skate career seriously, he stopped doing Grizzly completely. Years later, when he joined the team at Diamond Supply, he asked if he could distribute his griptape through them, and then slowly through Pudwill's promotion and word of mouth, Grizzly grip popped up everywhere. From there it expanded to clothing and accessories—and he even brought back the bear-shaped wax that started it all.

Many skate companies begin in unassuming ways: as a lark, as a crew, as an in-joke. Then through hard work, luck, ingenuity, and patience, they occasionally become legitimate brands. (Most, of course, fail to fully develop.) Shake Junt, another griptape brand that grew to include other products, was launched by pro skater (and hype man) Shane Heyl, who personally spray painted onto each roll the Shake Junt's loud yellow and green logo himself. Originally, Heyl told *The Nine Club*, "It had no meaning to becoming a company whatsoever. All that is right there is a bunch of friends putting some skating together for a video called Shake Junt. And then the movement kinda happened to [become] a crew." The name "Shake Junt" is a Southern euphemism for a strip club, and it also appears in the Three 6 Mafia song "Try Somethin.'"

The point is that for much of the history of skateboarding, companies were run by skaters, who did so not out of a desire to become rich (most of them wouldn't) but out of love and passion—and also to set themselves up for careers beyond being a pro skater. The shelf life of a pro skater is really short—and anyway the money isn't exactly setting anyone up for retirement—so former pros often pursue work within the industry to sustain themselves post-career. The entrance into skateboarding of corporations like Nike and Adidas, et al, has made skater-run brands harder to succeed.

Back to Taylor. Her Grizzly run was a success. Not only was the apparel as creative and fashionable as Taylor herself is, but it also proved that she could design. She incorporated her sensibility into the pieces, which somehow manage to combine the casual with the ostentatious. The colors and angles and cuts are sharp, characterized by contrast and a simplicity in the patterns. As a whole there is no overarching aesthetic, other than Taylor's eclectic taste. The pieces were hoodies and sweatpants and bodysuits, the kind of thing, Taylor told The Berrics at the time, "that I could skate in but also hang out in, and also be lazy in." The clothes look dope, but they are not meant to remain pristine. You're supposed to skate in them. And the other pertinent quality of the Grizzly run is that they are designed for women. In the past, much of the skate gear aimed at women were simply the regular designs in a typically "girly" colorway. In the 90s, there was a rad, but short-lived, girl skate brand called Poot!, which you might remember for its "Girls Kick Ass" shirt that became really popular. And while some brands have put out some cool and thoughtful apparel designed for women, skateboarding's default aesthetic still skews male. Taylor's run had sports bras and midriff-exposing tops.

At this point Taylor got herself a manager (whose agency I had to go through in order to set up our interview), which propelled her into a new level of sponsorship and exposure. Those early $200 jobs made way for much higher paying gigs. Under Amour paid her seven grand for a post. Converse paid her five. Ever the ambitious sort, Taylor wasn't satisfied with simply making more money. "I was like, 'This is cool, but I want to be doing bigger things. I don't want to just be doing Instagram posts.'" So she was particularly thrilled by an opportunity presented to her by Jansport, who "ended up doing this whole campaign with me. They took me to Coachella last year. They gave me multiple bags that I still use every single day. They gave me a budget for a very nice AirBnB. Like, it was so much fun." That one paid her $10,000.

If you feel like Taylor's being gauche by mentioning the amounts she was paid, just know that I asked her to specifically provide me with these numbers. Money is something that people in skateboarding don't tend to talk about, mostly because most people in the industry don't make much of it. Companies don't pay their skaters well, and they often treat they're salaried staff just as cheaply. If brands are going to expect their riders to film, travel, enter contests, post on social media, and generally go all-out, then they have to be able to pay a living wage. There is no NBA-like organization in skateboarding, no centralized, funded, and lucrative center to employ skaters as professionals. Instead, it's all contract work, which means skaters make their money from sponsorships, which in effect makes skaters more like models than athletes. To be sure, some NBA players make more money from Nike and Reebok, etc. than they do from their teams, but even the non-superstars still earn a living by playing. Skaters earn their living by, essentially, modeling clothes. What Taylor does is social media influencing, yes, but it's also no different than what skaters have to do. They all get paid by companies to be seen wearing their clothes, riding their boards, or using their products.

Money should be more openly discussed, because allowing such a topic to remain unspoken benefits the companies and not the skaters. Taylor generously informed me as to the particulars of her work, which I greatly appreciate, but the mention of money was my idea, not hers.

Since her foray into high-paying promotion—which also includes Victoria's Secret, Puma, and Calvin Klein—Taylor has been on two missions: to launch her own clothing line and to continue progressing as a skater. At the time of our conversation, she'd spent about $10,000 on four or five samples. "I'm not interested in printing t-shirts," she told me. "I'm not interested in anything of that sort. I am interested in high-end quality, good tailoring." But that doesn't mean expensive. "The majority of my demographic, my followers— they're skateboarders. So I'm trying to figure out what's missing in the market of really high-end quality products, but also create a price point so that every single person that follows me and supports me can afford it."

Taylor possesses a kind of confidence that I can imagine might turn a person off, but it's also the kind you would need in order to do what she does. I don't mean to say she's arrogant—only that she doesn't question the potential success of her ambitions. "I am going to be a famous fashion designer," she told me. "I am going to have a really well-known clothing brand. It's going to happen, but it's not going to happen today, it's not going to happen tomorrow. The only thing I can do right now is think positive, think it's going to happen and do what I can now. And that's the best thing I can do." She has, in other words, the confidence of a skateboarder. Skaters don't master tricks today, or tomorrow, but after many weeks, months, years of practice. But you can't progress—or, more accurately, convince yourself to persevere—if you don't believe that you'll get there. Taylor believes she will get there, and because of that she very likely will.

As a woman in a (for now) male-dominated field, she's been forced to endure a lot of bullshit, a lot of unnecessary hate and threats and violence, and she's gained some hard-earned wisdom from it. At one point she said to me, when talking about how difficult it is for her to trust the men she meets, "It's scary because a lot of men don't show their true colors until something is taken away from them." That is quite an insight, an observation that's paradigmatic of our current culture. In order for our world to improve, men must lose some of their power, and many men are not happy about that. The backlash against gains in gender equality is predictable (it's similar to the way white people often respond to developments of racial equity), but it's also tragic. Men will hurt and abuse and kill many women on their way out the doors of power, because something is being taken from them, and those are their true colors. But skateboarding is overdue for a complete overhaul. And Taylor is a part of that. As she puts it: "We've seen a man do everything on a skateboard. Have we seen a woman do everything on a skateboard? No, we have not."

5 BEAUTIFUL MUTANTS

On his grandmother's birthday, May 31st, 2012, Gary Rogers launched *Skateline*, a weekly parody of TV news focused on the world of skateboarding and driven by the charm, humor, and the sometimes savage but mostly good-natured commentary of its host. A typical episode will last between three and four minutes. Its opening music perfectly mimics the "breaking news" intros news channels used in decades past, replete with a typewriter sample, which plays over an image of a silhouetted Rogers sitting at a desk and facing the camera like a newscaster, with a wall of screens behind him that look like a mix between the cliché newsroom backdrop of TV news and the realm of the Architect in *The Matrix Reloaded*. The title of the show flies into frame and lands just above Rogers's head. At the exact moment the music crescendos, we flash cut to Rogers in a suit, a stack of papers in front of him, who invariably says, "Welcome, everybody, to another episode of *Skateline* NBD and—" At this point Rogers jumps right into it, without delay, finishing this opening line with a hyperbolic description of a skate clip from Instagram or YouTube. Then, he covers the latest in skate news, which usually focuses on video parts, skaters turning pro or changing sponsors, and occasionally serious stuff (like a death in the industry or, in a notable episode, the Black Lives Matter movement). As of this writing, nearly nine years after its premiere, Rogers has yet to miss a single week.

Rogers grew up in the Bay Area, and as a young skate rat he hung out at Metro Skateshop in Concord, a city just northeast of San Francisco. Joel Jutagir opened the shop in 1999, and it became a staple of the local scene and a frequent stop for touring pros and ams. Jutagir extended his presence in skateboarding with his YouTube channel, Metro Skateboarding. Jutagir recognized in Rogers the talent and approach that he would come to be known for.

"Joel was like, 'Kid, I rock with your energy,'" Rogers told me over Zoom. "'You always come into the shop. You're part of the shop. You're family. Let's do something on YouTube together.'" Shortly after, Jutagir came to Rogers with the idea for a faux-news show.

YouTube in 2013 had yet to become the skateboarding juggernaut it is now, but having a presence on the site was necessary. Skate companies—who are so dependent on video for their identity, marketing, and revenue—initially viewed YouTube as an extension of their video outreach. Full-length videos were still sold as DVDs, Blu-Rays, or digital downloads, while YouTube existed as a portal for advertising. *Pretty Sweet*, the Girl/Chocolate video by Ty Evans, Cory Weincheque, and Spike Jonze, was probably the last skate event video sold on its own. Released in 2012, *Pretty Sweet* was the culmination of years of filming and was in all respects a big-budget undertaking: it has special effects, celebrity cameos, high production value, and an Academy Award-winning co-director. Premieres were held in numerous cities across America (I went to one in Boston, where Kenny Anderson was also in attendance. Afterward, a ton of skaters hit up a nearby bar, and I found myself drunkenly talking Anderson's ear off, during which he was generously polite when he totally didn't have to be.) YouTube, at the time, was seen as a force to combat, because it was in Girl/Chocolate's interest to stop people from uploading the video or parts from it, since their profits came from purchases, not views.

In subsequent years, YouTube shifted from the extension of a platform to the entire platform. Shared revenue from advertisers allows channels to earn income while simultaneously marketing products. Metro Skateboarding, Jutagir's channel for his shop, was one of the early successes of YouTube skateboarding, and its popularity was due in part to creative ideas like *Skateline* and investment in talent like Rogers.

Rogers's persona on *Skateline* is exactly that: a persona. "I've created a character," he said. "My name is Gary Rogers. That's who I am, but it's still a character. And that character likes to poke fun. But he's not malicious."

During our two-and-a-half-hour conversation over Zoom, this statement was proven true. Gary on Skateline is a loud, quip-a-second comedian, who has this hilarious ability to say a stream of funny, sometimes free-associative jokes, all under his breath. Watching the show, I am sometimes reminded of Dave Chappelle's delivery on *Chappelle's Show*— specifically the sketch where Chappelle plays a black version of then-President Bush. Giving a press conference at the White House during the height of the Iraq War, Chappelle's Black Bush says, in a line where the speed and rhythm of the delivery increases as it moves along:

> U.N, you got a problem with that? You know what you should do? You should sanction me, sanction me with your army. Oh! Wait a minute! You don't have an army! I guess that means you need to shut the fuck up. That's what I would do if I had no army, I would shut the fuck up. Shut. The. Fuck. Up! That's right, Kofi Annan. You think I'm going to take orders from an African? You might speak sixteen languages, but you gonna need 'em when you in Times Square selling fake hats. I know Gucci when I see it, n***a, I'm rich.

The way Chappelle moves through the logic of this, the way he punctuates his points with vocal emphasis, the way he mutters through some of the words, particularly the last line—it is pure Rogers. Chappelle, of course, has his influences, too; this style can be seen in the comedy of Will

Smith and Chris Rock and Eddie Murphy and Richard Pryor. In this way, Rogers carries on a tradition of black comedy. But for Rogers, the bedrock of *Skateline* is Chappelle.

"He was gone when we started *Skateline*," he said. "He disappeared for a long time, so I feel like I tried to give that persona off through what I missed, you know, as far as my favorite person." Despite this, Rogers doesn't consider himself a comedian. Or, rather, he doesn't want to call himself a comedian; he'll let other people do that for him. This goes back to the discussion I had with Mark Waters about Kyle Walker's "No Other Way" part, the common reluctance in skateboarding to self-define, to take credit for one's accomplishments.

When I brought this up to Rogers, he said something similar about Walker, albeit with more specificity. "It's the survival that makes him tweak the way he does. If you go to some of Kyle's spots, you can die . . . And the fact that some of those clips are four or five trips. Some of those clips are after an injury."

Then Rogers brings up Bastien Salabanzi, a French pro who made a huge impact in Flip's *Sorry* video in 2002, doing tricks that would still be impressive and slow-mo worthy, even in 2022. After that video came out, Salabanzi became a pro, at fifteen. At twenty-one, he left his sponsors and returned to France, burned out from years of travel and filming. He still skated and still entered the occasional contest, but now the pressure was off—he returned to the fun. Near the end of the 2010s, Salabanzi skated in a contest in Paris, which played out in a jam session format, meaning that participants all skated the park at the same time for a specified amount of time, and whoever did the raddest shit in that period would be declared the winner. There is a video on YouTube entitled "Bastien Salabanzi Show" (a play on the contest's title, The Tony Hawk Show), and it is something to behold. It begins with a montage of some of the other skaters, who land some high-level tricks. There's a decently-sized six-stair with a rail and hubba, and a big five-block (a block is just a large stair, the equivalent of two or three stairs combined, so a five block would be around the size of a ten- or twelve-stair, give or take). A skater 180s and fakie ollies the four-block; someone else frontside flips it. Another dude fakie frontside flips the six-stair, and some tricks go down on the handrail—solid stuff all around.

But then Salabanzi appears, and he destroys the place. He does tricks I've only seen done a handful of times, ever, like a double-flip frontside boardslide down the handrail. Let me see if I can articulate just why that specific trick is so remarkable: double flips take a while to finishing flipping, which means you have to pop higher and time the land just right. When I double-flip, my knees tuck into my chest as I wait to land, and when I do, I often slam my feet down onto the board, making sure to stop its flipping in its tracks. Doing a frontside boardslide down an inclined obstacle requires a somewhat soft touch. If you slam too hard onto the rail, you'll slip out and fall on your face. So the fact that Salabanzi was able to double-flip onto a rail without crashing down too hard and still maintain enough control to complete the slide—I can't even fathom it. When he lands these tricks, Salabanzi makes numerous gestures of self-celebration: pointing toward the enormous, looming video monitor for the replay; shrugging Michael Jordan-style; yelling exultations; bowing to the audience. He's like a rock star.

"Looking back at the footage and stuff," Salabanzi said on an episode of the podcast *The Nine Club*, "I can definitely understand from like an outside perspective that people thought I was literally insane . . . I was like over-expressive and like the energy was up to the roof." He's talking about this obscure contest nearly a decade later because his antics during it became notorious—in both positive and negative ways. To some, he was cool; to others, cocky. But the lingering effects of one outburst of self-congratulatory exuberance remained memorable to skaters, even years and years on. (When I brought up the topic of self-celebration to Jonathan Mehring, he too brought up Salabanzi.) Here's the thing, though: the real reason for Salabanzi's hype was that his older brother was in the audience. He'd always looked up to his brother and clamored at the opportunity to show him what he could in person, instead of in a video. Having spent many years living and skating in the US, away from his family, now that he lived in France again, he could impress his older brother, a younger sibling's dream. In the clip, Salabanzi even stops midway through the session, gives his board and the shirt off his back to a random kid (another rock-star move), and goes and sits with his brother in the audience. The pride in his face is wonderful, once you know the context. His excitement is wholly personal, and he's not celebrating himself but rather his brother—the degree to which he's stoked about landing something is directly related to how thrilled he is that his brother got to see it.

This is what is left out of such judgements: the details. I never knew that Salabanzi's brother attended that contest, just like I don't know anything about the specifics of Kyle Walker's clips. But even when I found out that Walker has no such stories, that he's just hyped on himself and that's it—even then, there wouldn't be anything wrong with it, because a primary component of skateboarding, whether we want to admit it or not, is showing off. When there is a crowd, or, like Salabanzi, a specific person in the crowd, skaters try harder shit; they take risks, and they commit more readily.

As a teenager, I thrived on people watching me. At skateparks, for instance, I landed harder tricks and landed them faster than I would have if I'd been alone. The sound of an entire skatepark going nuts over something you did—there is nothing like it. How many times in your life have you gotten applause? How often do people bang objects onto metal and shout and whistle and jump in response to you? The only other examples of fervid applause I've ever experienced were when I performed on a stage, and even then it wasn't the same kind of rousing and raucous explosion. But it speaks to the nature of skateboarding as an activity, the fact that the only comparison I have for how my skating has been received is from performances. Skateboarding is a performance; not always and not entirely, but it is fundamental.

When you look at skateboarding this way, Salabanzi's and Walker's triumphant boasts are not only understandable but quite fitting (during the writing of this book, Salabanzi put out a video part entitled "Not So Sorry"; good for him). Think of the way athletes commemorate a great play: the end zone dance; the bat toss. Think of Dwyane Wade hopping onto the scorer's table after hitting the game-winner against the Bulls. We eat this shit up. And we do so because we're keenly aware of how rarefied such talent is. Wade has every right to shout, "This is our house!" to a cheering crowd because, well, only he (and a tiny handful of others) could have done what he just did. Obviously, if Wade walked around treating everything he did like this, he'd be an unbearable asshole—but winning an NBA game at the buzzer certainly merits an ostentatious display.

Of course, all of these examples are men. The way culture views an athlete's celebrations is totally gendered. It's much more acceptable for a man to be arrogant and self-confident than it is for a woman to be. The US Women's Soccer team was heavily criticized for what some referred to as excessively celebrating their win over Thailand in the first round of the World Cup in 2019. Critics said it wasn't classy because they won 13-0. In 1999, another US Women's Soccer player, Brandi Chastain, stirred a fervor of controversy when she took off her shirt after scoring a decisive goal against China. She wore a sports bra underneath, which much of the world decided was not enough. These criticisms can also be racial: Serena Williams's celebrations have often disconcerted the tennis world's typically white commentators.

Skateboarding, as we've seen, also has issues with gender, but for now I want to focus on its general attitude toward etiquette. There are a good number of unspoken rules in skateboarding. Example: when Gary Rogers opens his show with the phrase, "Welcome, everybody, to *Skateline* NBD," what does he mean by NBD? NBD stands for Never Been Done—which has two related but distinct meanings: tricks no one has done before generally, and tricks no one has done before at specific spots. It is considered taboo to film yourself doing the same trick at the same spot as somebody else. If you go to Hollywood High to skate the sixteen-stair handrail, it's acceptable to film yourself doing shit past skaters have done, but only for non-skate-part purposes, like posting on Instagram or playing during the credits like an outtake. If you want to skate the Hollywood sixteen (as it's referred to) in your part, you've got to do something heretofore unseen.

Other nonverbal prohibitions. At a skatepark, wait your turn, as jumping in out of order is called "snaking," a dysphemism that has been around since I was a kid. In games of SKATE (which is just HORSE for skateboarders), it's customary to start with easier tricks before launching into the really difficult ones. You're not supposed to use the same song as someone else for your video part. When carrying your board, grab it by the nose or tail, or hold it perpendicularly with your hand gripping the center of the deck—all of which is to say you never, *never*, carry it by the truck. This is called "mall-grabbing" and it functions like a litmus test: real skaters never do it; fake-ass ones almost always do.

The point here is that skateboarding has developed categorical imperatives like any other culture. These are—to use some more arcane vocab—social mores. Etiquette. Which doesn't exactly sound menacing, does it?

Back to Rogers.

I am reminded here that Rogers is intimately involved with the world of skateboarding. He doesn't just co-write and host *Skateline*, he is an active member of the skate community. He's hosted or participated in numerous events put on by *Thrasher*. He's been a commentator during the X-Games. He even had a few skate clips in Illegal Civ's popular 2020 full-length *Godspeed*, and they were not too shabby. You can spot Rogers in the background at contests, parties, and various other skating activities. He's what's known as a fixture. Which means he has insider insights about the skate world, a fact made clearer by the outlets on which his show has aired.

Although Metro Skateboarding launched *Skateline*, it only played there for a few episodes. Next, it was picked up by Ride Channel, which was, for a number of years, the most popular skateboarding channel on YouTube. It specialized in click-bait-style videos with titles like "Skateboarder Backflips Down 6 Stairs!!!" and "Cop Car Runs Over Skateboarder!!!" Tony Hawk appears in eight of their top ten most viewed videos. In a 2016 article on *Quarter Snacks*, Ride Channel is referred to as "the skateboarding BuzzFeed," which is a fair enough assessment, although that's a relatively ironic dig from an entity whose most popular feature—a daily Top Ten trick reel—deliberately models itself after ESPN's *SportsCenter*.

But these accusatory comparisons to mainstream media are both a telling representation of the ascent of skateboarding in popular culture and a damning marker of its cultural pacification. The more skateboarding becomes a part of pop culture, the more it mimics the cultural monoliths against which it originally rebelled: sports, corporations, the wealthy. In the past decade or so, companies like Nike, Adidas, and Converse have thrown in their primly mass-produced hats into the ring. Red Bull takes it one step further: they sponsor an elite squad of skaters, pay them handsomely, and require them to wear gaudy, bright blue and red hats that undo whatever cool vibe a skater's outfit attempts to give off. Even high-end brands like Louis Vuitton have gotten in on pre-Olympic action, so that when the international windfall that the most watched global sports event will inevitably bring rains down over skaters, Louis Vuitton can snatch up as much of that heavenly manna before it ever touches the hand of an actual skateboarder. Vuitton, in 2020, released a $1,190 skate shoe—which to me feels like a bit of a "fuck you" to the spirit of menacing rebels. Rogers, I discovered, disagrees.

"I love clothes," he told me. "I love fashion. I appreciate it. I love looking nice." For him there is a distinction between the sports brands and the fashion brands. "In my eyes, these aren't the worlds of competition. So the sport coming here is what I don't like, because it makes the idea that one person is better than another in our field, which isn't true. But the fashion thing lets everybody try to look good. And that's what I like, that everybody can try to look nice and do their thing. I like that."

I had never considered it this way before. To me there really isn't a difference between Nike and Louis Vuitton—they're both wealthy companies shamelessly trying to extract any profit from a rising subculture, which ultimately takes away from the skaters. The profit doesn't trickle down.

But there is yet another side to this. A sponsored skateboarder—whether pro or amateur—is technically a contractor rather than an employee, which means sponsors don't have to provide health insurance or even guaranteed salaries. If a skater suffers an injury that will require months or even years of recuperation, a sponsor can drop them at any moment, leaving them without an income source just as they're about to incur the extreme costs of rehab (this can include surgeries, physical therapy, and the loss of time). These contractual dynamics have been this way for as long as skateboarding has existed, mostly because these brands never made very much money. They couldn't afford to hire skaters as employees with salaries and benefits; they barely made ends meet. Multi-billion-dollar companies like Nike and Red Bull can afford to provide their skate team with necessary medical care for a healthy recovery. Of course, they're still all contractors, and Nike still drops skaters like candy wrappers, but the ones they do retain are treated well. For example, Jamie Foy, a pro for Red Bull, explained on *The Nine Club* that the energy drink brand gives him access to a cryo-chamber, a form of physical therapy that immerses you in extremely cold temperatures to help reduce soreness. It's the high-tech equivalent of an ice bath. For an NBA or NFL athlete, such amenities are a matter of course, but for a skateboarder, even a top-level one, they are luxuries.

The corporatization of skateboarding, then, presents the same Faustian compromises as it does in any field: it will fill your pockets as it drains your soul. But here's the rub: what if the soul of skateboarding—by which I mean its founding ethos, not its actual, objective quintessence—was wrong to begin with? What if its anti-authoritarian, skate-and-destroy philosophy wasn't, in the end, inclusive enough? Is it possible that the unexpected consequence of corporate intrusion is that skateboarding has grown less niche and more universally appealing? Does it matter whether skating is popular? Does it have to be an elite community in order for it to feel special?

I remember vividly the growing awareness, acceptance, and even appreciation that came in the wake of Tony Hawk's 900 at the X-Games in 1999. I was fourteen when it happened and over the next few years—as strangers approached me on the street asking, "Can you 900?" or brought up Tony Hawk with such smug self-satisfaction—I resented skating's burgeoning status. Being a skater was what made me *me*; it was integral to my identity. And when something that makes you feel special starts to become ubiquitous, the shift can seem like a theft. It brings to mind the refrain from *The Incredibles*: "As soon as everyone's special, then nobody is." My bitterness toward skating's growth was, in retrospect, wrong headed for a variety of reasons, but the most important one is this: my identity is made up of much more than my activities: I am more than a skater, more than a writer, more than a guitar-playing, dog-owning reader. I am those things; but they speak to surfaces rather than essences. But at fourteen, I couldn't disassociate the things I loved from how and why I loved them. Two people can adore identical passions and yet be completely different people. This is an obvious truth, but at fourteen I had yet to learn it.

I wasn't the only one who needed to learn this lesson. For a long time, the gatekeepers of skateboarding were resistant to its expansion. Recall the how intense the opposition was for Mark Waters and company as they tried to get skateboarding into the Olympics.

In the past two decades, the sight of the *Thrasher* logo emblazoned on some non-skater's T-shirts surprise no one. Skateboarding aesthetic has bled into the mainstream, so a few of its totemic emblems appear divorced from their referents. For Rogers, this is a half-assed gesture. "It's like, you could come over here. You could do this. This is fun. Join us. Join the cult." And what bothers him is a matter of commitment, of *earning* the right to rock skate gear. "They just want to be accepted by that group of people so bad and feel included in that aspect of life without trying to come feel this pain. Come feel some pain. Come break something. Come get hurt. That's that barbaric *Thrasher* soul that I live by."

It's appropriate that Rogers embodies the *Thrasher* spirit because he has become one of its most prominent figureheads. Since its inception, *Thrasher*'s spokesperson and mascot was Jake Phelps, the longtime editor-in-chief and, in many ways, the leader of all skateboarding. This dude was just out there, in the streets, screaming and yelling and jumping up and down and getting everybody psyched, like the emcee of skateboarding. But he also tore people down if he didn't like them. He could be caustic, fractious, grudging. But no one in skateboarding has or will ever again hold as much power and influence. Phelps joined *Thrasher* in the 80s but he became the EIC in 1993 and retained that role until his death in 2019. During his tenure, *Thrasher* became the preeminent tastemaker in the skate scene. It established and raised to a level of importance a yearly award called Skater of the Year, known by its acronym SOTY. In the 90s, the honor was bestowed on whomever Phelps and the mag thought killed it that year. Its process for picking a winner was unknown, and it hadn't yet reached the degree of significance he would eventually obtain, so no skaters competed for it deliberately. How could they have? But YouTube and social media and the always-connected world of skating has made it possible for skaters to go after SOTY. How *Thrasher* names a winner remains a mystery (although they've included a fan vote system that suggests that popularity has something to do with it), but there are clear factors that tip a decision one way or the other: video parts, contest wins, general ubiquity. Mason Silva, who won SOTY for 2020, put out four video parts his winning year. *Four*. That is absurd. It's also what it takes now to win.

No amount of striving will ever be enough for certain skaters, however, as a few skaters, most notably Nyjah Huston, will simply never be given the honorific. Huston—who has won more contests than any contemporary pro—is too mainstream, too athlete-like, for *Thrasher* to ever put their stamp of approval on him. Sure, their vitriol toward him lessened over the years, as evidenced by Phelps appearing in numerous videos with Huston, talking him up, describing him as "the real deal." If there's one thing Phelps respected above all, it was dedication to skateboarding, and Huston is probably the most assiduous skater alive. But there were a couple of years when it was clear that Huston was gunning for SOTY—particularly 2013, when Huston released, in December (the final month of the year is when many of the best video parts are dropped, like films competing for Oscars), "Fade to Black," a part so transparently aimed at *Thrasher* that, even though Huston's skating was incredible, its blatant advocacy tainted its reception. Huston used the Metallica song after which it is named, which a) must have cost a fortune, and b) seems incongruous to Huston's aesthetic, since every other part he's ever put out features hip hop. There is nothing wrong with Huston wanting SOTY—every skater wants it; the problem was that he was among the first to noticeably pursue it, which seemed shameful. Nowadays it's commonplace. Mason Silva didn't put out four video parts in order to *not* win SOTY. It crossed his mind even if it didn't fully dictate his plans.

The point, though, is that *Thrasher*'s opinion carries a great deal of currency in skateboarding. It is, after all, the only print magazine still standing—*Transworld, Skateboarder, Big Brother* are either dead or in a different format. *Thrasher*'s circulation is something like 100,000, so it's not exactly setting the world on fire with subscriptions only. No, *Thrasher* has maintained relevance by virtue of its online presence. Like Metro Skateboarding, *Thrasher* pivoted their focus toward short-form video. Their YouTube page has 2.6 million followers; their Instagram sits at 6.6 million. Now *that* is reach. Not only does *Thrasher* release video parts from the top pro skaters, but they also have recurring segments like "My War," a show in which skaters tell the arduous story of a particularly harrowing trick, which regularly yields a million-plus views. Another popular regular feature they have is a show they picked up in 2014 and still release every week to this day: *Skateline*.

Thrasher is based in San Francisco, so like Metro it's a good fit for Rogers. But there's also, of course, its legacy as *the* skate mag and its notorious editor. "That's my guy," Rogers said of the Phelper (as he's often referred to). "That persona of like, 'I don't really care, embodying like that'—it's like, yeah, he did bash the little famous kids when they were younger, he did live like that, but if you really talked to him, you know he didn't hate you. But he was just being like, 'You're a famous little shit. You're not better than any of us. You're one of us. Remember that.'"

And true to Phelps's form, *Thrasher*'s content is made for adults: their videos feature cursing and drinking and drugs and a general fuck-authority vibe. This is fitting for what they advocate for, but on the other end of the YouTube spectrum are channels like Braille Skateboarding (5.7 million subscribers) and Andy Schrock's Revive (4.3 million), both of which market to young kids and novices.

"Shit is proven," Rogers said of these channels. He continued:

> It is proven that the company that makes the most money in skateboarding is not a company that has an ad in the biggest magazine of all time. It only exists on YouTube and sells products. As a skateboard company you don't have to follow any of the rules because it's focused on the youth. They made their own wheels. They made their own hardware. They made their own wax. They made their own ramps. They made their own warehouses.

It's a tactic that Rogers believes that "skateboarding missed." Skaters were too busy being badasses; they neglected a huge demographic, or maybe they simply didn't know how to market successfully to them. Braille and Revive very much know how.

Take Revive, for instance. It began with Andy Schrock's personal YouTube page, which after a rough beginning started to grow in popularity. His videos were accessible, funny, and generically appealing. One day, he tossed out the idea of doing a limited run of boards to see if his subscribers would buy them. It was called Revenge and the initial run sold out. So he did it another time, and another, until finally the idea of starting a proper company became impossible to resist. He had to change the name because of a copyright claim from another brand, so he went with Revive, as it sounds similar to Revenge but is also a wink to reemerging from a setback. The business grew and grew and eventually Revive set up a warehouse for their products and sold them directly to their customers through their website. This practice simply wasn't done in skateboarding before.

Here's how it had always worked: skate companies sold their products to skate shops, or to distributors who then sold them to skate shops, and then skate shops sold to skaters. Skate shops served as intermediaries for a few reasons. First, they functioned as meeting spots for skaters. In the 90s, skateboarding wasn't popular, and without the internet and a dearth of skateparks, skaters' only way of finding community was at a shop. Though of course they differ in a lot of aspects, certain features of a skate shop are pretty much universal: a looming wall of decks; racks of shirts; a glass-encased counter filled with bearings, wheels, stickers, tools, and videos; a vise for setting up boards (a service shops provide); and a sofa parked in front of a wall-mounted TV playing the latest full-length or maybe a 411 (a "video magazine," which is a subscription-based series released quarterly). They were designed to be hangouts. Many skaters, like Rogers at Metro, discovered their people via shops.

The other reason for these brick-and-mortar proxies is disambiguation. Skateboards come with a lot of stuff, and each thing is measured by different criteria. Boards, for instance, are measured in inches, but also judged by shape; you can have two 8.25' decks with wholly distinct forms: varying degrees of concave, smaller or larger noses and tails, weight, length, etc. The measurement of trucks is a confounding fuck-all, to be honest. Some brands use millimeters, others use their own systems that have explanations but aren't useful for consumers. Wheels come in sizes ranging from 48mm to 60mm (wheels in the 60+mm range are used for longboards or mega ramp skating). Then there are bearings, which have no measurements at all, and hardware and grip tape and, optionally, riser pads (which go under your trucks to raise them a bit higher and give you more pop) and rails (which are two plastic strips fashioned onto the bottom of the deck, lining the edges, making boardslides extra slippery and providing grips for grabs). A kid (and their parents) can be excused for being a bit overwhelmed by all these choices. The permutations alone are mind boggling. Skate shops— and specifically their knowledgeable staff––can offer some much-needed clarification.

Andy Schrock, by skipping this essential step, challenged a long-held paradigm of the skate industry. On *The Nine Club*, Heath Brinkley, a veteran filmer and the executive vice president of Primitive Skateboarding, discussed the strange fact that the price of skateboard decks hasn't increased alongside inflation, reducing the profit margins for boards more and more. "Any brand, if they really wanted to, could be like, 'Well, you know what I sell you wholesale boards for? I'm going to put that online at that cost.' Any brand could do that. And let's be honest, Revive does that; $38 boards all day long. And I don't agree with that. It doesn't make sense for me to undercut these partnerships I have with these shops." A consequence of Schrock's business tactics is that Revive isn't exactly a respected brand in skateboarding.

But they are one of the most successful. Revive and Braille market themselves very effectively to kids. "There are so many kids starting to skateboard today," Rogers said, "and when it looks safe, they're going to show their mom, like, Hey look at this guy on YouTube that isn't cursing, that has helmets on, braces, pads, and you're in that household, you're going to be like, 'Alright I'm gonna buy my kid this funny thing he wants, this toy,' and then you watch all this YouTube stuff. It's parental advice. It's all PG, you know?" Revive and Braille is sort of like YA literature—the quality is no different but the content and the packaging make clear the age group it's designed for, and signal to parents its appropriateness. Plus, Braille and Revive's videos feature fun, click-bait-style stunts, like skateboards made out of any material you can imagine: glass, metal, TVs, iPads, whatever. Braille now has a line of fingerboards based on these recurring videos that are on sale at Target. Schrock does a series with his son Ryden in which they skate together, play games, explore nature, and just generally engage in some wholesome father-son stuff. These channels are fun and harmless and very, very popular.

How popular? I don't know exact numbers (one source I spoke to thinks their valuation is somewhere in the vicinity of $40 million), but I know this: Braille's founder, Aaron Kyro, who is also the face of the company and appears in many of its videos, is a Scientologist, and in a 2019 donor list in Scientology's *Impact* magazine, Kyro is listed as a "Silver Meritorious with Honors," which means he donated at least $750,000 to the organization. Without even attempting to extrapolate a firm estimate of his wealth, it's clear that Kyro has lots of money, which in turn suggests that Braille rakes it in.

These entities—Braille and Revive—are introducing an entire generation of children to skateboarding, so in five to ten years, when those kids have come of age, Braille and Revive will be the norm rather than the exceptions. The legacy of *Thrasher*, which has functioned as the legacy of skateboarding for decades now, will be replaced by a much more wholesome and inoffensive one.

I'm not trying to argue whether this is good or bad, only that it's true. *Thrasher*'s guiding ethos isn't limited to the magazine. Brands like Anti-Hero and FA (Fucking Awesome) and Hockey and Fancy Lad, et al., carry the torch for misanthropic rebellion, and their collective influence is considerable. But this is a numbers game, and these companies don't have shit on Braille and Revive, nor are they interested in that level of power. You can't be anti-authoritarian while aiming to become an authority. The consequence of this power imbalance will be a major shift in what skateboarding is.

Rogers, for his part, views what Revive is doing as fundamentally no different than any other skate company. "I realized the reason why I don't attack them, like Revive and those dudes—I make fun; I poke fun at everybody, 'cause you know, it's still cornball—but I don't attack [Schrock] because he's for the kids. All you can defend is the youth. You know, I was a part of that. It was not that long ago. You know, ten years ago, eleven years ago, I was a kid."

Rogers grew up in Oakland, in what he said was "not the best area," and his childhood wasn't exactly easy. But at fourteen, he took a Razor scooter to a skatepark near him and realized after fifteen minutes that it was too easy. "So I took it back home and I grabbed my skateboard and ever since fourteen that's what I've been doing every day. The scooter was just too easy. I literally rode it over there for fifteen minutes, grabbed my board, came back, tried that and failed a hundred times. And I was like: 'I like how I can't do this.'" Skateboarding gave him a necessary component to an ambitious life: a challenge. And that challenge helped him leave the past behind, dropped like a scooter that wasn't difficult enough. "Everything that might've happened yesterday," he said, "it's not sitting here with me. Like, I got better. I did what I wanted to do."

So, when he thinks of the notion that only gnarly, hard-living misfits can participate in skating and that the more innocuous and milquetoast companies like Revive aren't rad enough to be included, Rogers had this to say: "I always try to tell people, you don't have to live as much life as I have. Feel me? Life is scary as fuck. It is. It's horrifying. But I always tell people, you ain't gotta do that and you don't have to do that."

All you have to do is skate.

EPILOGUE

THIS IS SKATEBOARDING

"Twenty years ago, this wasn't a common idea," Mark Waters said to me in our very first meeting. "No one twenty years ago, I think, really said, 'Skateboarding is about *this*,' and it was just accepted. People would try to define it, and it was always argued. It wasn't until about twelve maybe fifteen years ago that this became accepted. But for me, I've determined that the one-word answer to what skateboarding is about: progression."

Progression. This, to me, is the essence of skateboarding. Very few people who get on a skateboard and learn how to ride around on a few ramps and down the street would remain satisfied with this, even if it was their initial goal. Skaters want to get better, skate faster, do bigger shit, develop a smoother style, learn new tricks. It is part and parcel with the culture. And it's an individual thing, too, something every skater seems to innately grasp. Let's say there are two skaters at a busy skatepark. One of them is a novice, the other a ripper. The novice tries to kickflip over a fun box, and it's a struggle, but eventually the novice sticks it. The ripper, however, for whom kickflipping the fun box is no big deal, in a line, almost as an afterthought, kickflips the fun box too. The crowd at the park will cheer for the novice and not the ripper, because everyone can discern the level of difficulty of any given skater's skillset. Skaters know that for the novice, the kickflip was an accomplishment, something to be celebrated, whereas the ripper's kickflip is a mere matter of course, no celebration necessary. Now, when the ripper pulls out some really crazy shit—the kind of thing no one else at the park could come close to—the applause and cheers will be louder than they were for the novice, but there is still an implicit understanding of contextual achievements.

Consider how tedious and unrewarding much of skating is. You try over and over to land a trick, a process involving pain, frustration, and a lot of time. No one who becomes a skater and continues to skate escapes the hours of toiling and failing it requires, much of it public—in front of friends, other skaters, strangers on the street, contest judges. This hazardous recreational activity demands a certain kind of personality, one willing to persevere through some painful and humiliating adversity.

It's no surprise that the subjects of this book are all self-motivated and ambitious people who've accomplished a lot on their own. Waters went from a teenage punk making zines to an Olympic coach. Suciu became one of the world's best skaters and still put himself through college; and last year he won *Thrasher's* Skater of the Year award. Mehring earned $100 for his first picture; eventually he published a glossy collection of photographs with *National Geographic*. Taylor has amassed quite a following on social media, something even her privileged upbringing couldn't guarantee her, and now she's debuting her own line of clothing. Rogers was a skate rat who now does commentary for events on ESPN. These are dedicated and hard-working entrepreneurs. All of their work is essentially freelance. In the case of Waters, he worked for a bunch of companies, which is to say he didn't just work his way up over the years through one brand but rather an entire industry. Skateboarding, among its many benefits, beats assiduity into you. Skaters progress tirelessly.

The world of skateboarding, on the other hand, isn't nearly as progressive as its practitioners. Skateboarders have a dismissive attitude toward careerism, and thus no unions, and no safeguards from what amounts to contract work. You're supposed to skate because you love it, not because it's financially rewarding—but can't we have both? This convention of having to go through some kind of rite of passage during which you're paid in exposure rather than dollars, so as to prove your dedication, is antiquated and, frankly, unethical. (The publishing industry commits similar breaches of economic immorality—if one freelance writer isn't willing to write something for little to no money, then the next one will.) Skaters are an ambitious lot, and they'd rather progress without pay than stop progressing on moral grounds, which the current system frequently exploits.

Though skateboarding has been characterized as a haven for misfits, it isn't always a welcoming community. It took a long time for Black skaters to feel comfortable in the scene; women have had a hard road trying to be accepted despite constant immaturity and misogyny; gay skaters have only recently begun to be out and open; and trans skaters face just as much discrimination and vitriol as they do in the culture at large. Skateboarding, as a headline from an article by pro Anthony Pappalardo phrases it, is not progressive.

The quality that makes so many individuals successful in skateboarding isn't as present when those individuals become a group. Skaters are all about progression; skateboarding as a whole, less so. Things have gotten better, of course, than they were in the previous decades. For instance, there's a wonderful pop-up project called Consent Is Rad, which promotes consent in the skate scene and offers support to victims and survivors. They hold events, collaborate with groups, brands, and skaters to further the cause.

On the financial side of things, Heath Brinkley and Ryan Clements, both veterans of the skate industry, founded Excel Management, an agency with the sole purpose of helping skaters navigate their careers: negotiating contracts, paying taxes, saving for the future, and just generally managing their money. Skaters have for a long time resisted professionalization, but such developments are necessary to protect the livelihood of our people. I understand being dubious about corporate sponsorship and heavily controlled organizations like the Olympics, but skateboarding needs some form of centralization, not to help giant companies make more money but to enhance the lives of skaters themselves.

As vast and ubiquitous skateboarding has become since its creation, we ain't seen nothin' yet. Skateboarding still has too much to show us, so we have to allow for that constant expansion. We have to be open to developments that challenge previously held ideas, to paradigm shifts and social reckonings, to new styles and new people. If skateboarding is perpetually progressing, then that means it will continue menacing the world as long as there are streets to ride on. As Taylor put it when I asked her what one word she thought captured skateboarding, "It's forever just moving at all speeds. Like it's never-ending. There's no endpoint to it. There's always more. It's infinite."

ACKNOWLEDGMENTS

First and foremost, this book exists because of Mark Waters, who provided me with invaluable wisdom and necessary contacts. He was a generous, garrulous, and great person. Skateboarding is what it is today because of him.

Thanks to my other interviewees: Mark Suciu, Jonathan Mehring, Victoria Taylor, and Gary Rogers, who all spent hours speaking to me, and did so honestly, openly, and generously.

Thanks to my family, for the many ways they assisted me through the writing of this book. My mother has done so much for me I don't even know how to properly show gratitude. My sister Sarah is the most encouraging person in my life. Thanks to my brothers, Graham and Adam; if they hadn't started skating, I never would have either. And thanks to my dad, who bought me my first board and who I now have the pleasure of working with every week.

Thanks to my skater friends from over the years: Ben Tolford, Matthew Woellert, Brian Wilburn, Eric Zimmerman, Larry Roshirt, Kris Kittell, Greg Chmura, Jordan Tolford, Mike May, and the late, great Zack Pahl.

To my editors, Christopher Schaberg, Ian Bogost, and Haaris Naqvi for stewarding this book from pitch to publication. Also, thanks to Clarise Quintero for her thorough and thoughtful copyediting.

Thanks to Summer Brennan, who, in the earliest stages, allowed me to look at her proposal for *High Heel*, her own contribution to the Object Lessons series. Her book is wonderful and brilliant, as is she.

Thanks to Kevin Marks of Look Back Library, who does amazing work for skateboarding history.

Thanks to writer friends whose conversations helped me through the last year and change: Merve Emre, Ireland Headrick, and Jon Browning.

Thanks to Quantico, who is just the greatest little guy in the world.

Finally: thanks to JoAnna Carpentier, Jackie Donley, and Lauren Utvich.

SELECTED BIBLIOGRAPHY AND SUGGESTED FURTHER READING

Baccigaluppi, John and Sonny Mayugba and Chris Carnel.
  *Declaration of Independents: Snowboarding, Skateboarding +
  Music: An Intersection of Cultures*. San Francisco: Chronicle
  Books, 2001.

Beachy, Kyle. *The Most Fun Thing: Dispatches from a Skateboard
  Life*. New York: Grand Central Publishing, 2021.

Blabac, Mike. *Blablac Photo: The Art of Skateboarding Photography*.
  Brooklyn: PowerHouse Books, 2009.

Borden, Iain. *Skateboarding and the City: A Complete History*.
  London: Bloomsbury Visual Arts, 2019.

Brooke, Michael. *The Concrete Wave: The History of Skateboarding*.
  Toronto: Warwick Publishing, 1999.

Farnsworth, Ward. *Farnsworth's Classical English Rhetoric*. Boston:
  David R. Godine, 2011.

Hawk, Tony, with Sean Mortimer. *Hawk: Occupation:
  Skateboarder*. New York: ReganBooks, 2000.

Hocking, Justin, et al (ed). *Life & Limb: Skateboarders Write from the Deep End*. Brooklyn: Soft Skull Press, 2004.

Louison, Cole. *The Impossible: Rodney Mullen, Ryan Sheckler, and the Fantastic History of Skateboarding*. Guilford, Connecticut: Lyons Press, 2011.

Malcolm, Janet. *Nobody's Looking at You: Essays*. New York: FSG, 2019.

Mehring, Jonathan. *Skate the World: Photographing One World of Skateboarding*. Washington, D.C.: National Geographic, 2015.

Mitchell, David. *Cloud Atlas*. New York: Random House, 2004.

Mullen, Rodney, with Sean Mortimer. *The Mutt: How to Skateboard and Not Kill Yourself*. New York: It Books, 2004.

Reda, Giovanni. *Demigods & Cosmic Children*. New York: OHWOW Books, 2010.

Ryan, Walker. *Top of Mason*. New York: Old Friends, 2020.

Full-length Skate Videos and Documentaries

Bones Brigade: An Autobiography (2012), dir. Stacy Peralta

Cheese and Crackers (2006), dir. Socrates Leal, Almost Skateboards.

Dogtown & Z-Boys (2001), dir. Stacy Peralta

The End (1998), dir. Jamie Mosberg, Birdhouse Skateboards

Godspeed (2020), dir. Davonte Jolly, Illegal Civ

The Man Who Souled the World (2007), dir. Mike Hill

Modus Operandi (2000), dir. Ty Evans and Jon Holland, Transworld

Origin (2010), dir. Joe Castrucci, Habitat Skateboards

The Search for Animal Chin (1987), dir. Stacy Peralta, Powell-Peralta

Sorry (2002), dir. Fred Mortagne (French Fred), Flip Skateboards
Stay Gold (2010), dir. Jon Miner and Mike Manzoori, Emerica
Streets on Fire (1989), dir. Howard Dittrich, Santa Cruz
   Skateboards

Websites

Jenkem—jenkemmag.com
Thrasher Magazine—thrashermagazine.com
Quartersnacks—quartersnacks.com

YouTube Channels

Dumb Data
Gifted Hater
Hawk vs. Wolf
iDabble Video Magazine
The Nine Club
Rad Rat Video

INDEX